# ALIENS BEFOR

## A Guide to the  future

# ALIENS BEFORE GENTLEMEN

## A Guide to the Future

### By Richard D. Hall

**Illustrations by Richard D. Hall**

**Richpl anet.net**
Publishing

First published 2008 by RICHPLANET.NET

First Edition

# Richp l anet.net

**www.richplanet.net**

ISBN 978-0-9560355-0-9

Published by RICHPLANET.NET Publishing

# Contents

# Acknowledgements

I am grateful to my mother and father who are second to none and have supported me not just in writing this book, but throughout my life in everything I have done.

My great friend Jeremy Wynne helped proof read the work whilst stationed in Afghanistan. His input was essential in getting the book to read fluently and make sense.

Thank you if you contributed your opinions to the book, I have used some of them in the final chapter.

My partner Kerry has helped and supported me enormously, and is not afraid to tell me when something is not right. She continues to manage all of the activities we are involved with, including radio interviews, press releases and the website.

Thank you.

# Foreword

Within this book I have used some technical terminology and have referred to certain people, organisations and incidents. If I consider that further explanation is needed, I have included an explanation in the index with a reference number contained in square brackets.

For example

**MJ12** [a secret government organisation, **20**]

You should be able to quickly find the explanation in the index using the index number. Everything in the reference section is important to the book and I would encourage readers to read this section in full. This section gives vital information which supports the overall ideas discussed.

iii

# 1. Introduction

Many people have asked, what is the point of this book? The answer goes something like this: If we consider all of the information that is currently known about aliens, **UFOs** [Unidentified Flying Objects, **01**], alien technology and alien politics, which I can assure you is very extensive, what information would be most useful to know now in order to best prepare us for the future. By the future I mean the time when the **disclosure** [**08**] of the facts about aliens is announced by our governments, or indeed by the aliens themselves. What I am attempting to do in this book is to disseminate all of the available information and give you, the reader, the bits that may be useful in the future.

The book is not, however, a prediction of the future. Many authors have tried in vivid science fiction books to give us their vision of the future and the perils that may await us. Inevitably they all get it wrong. My approach will be different. We have all seen television programmes made in the 1950s which have attempted to portray what life would be like in the 1980s. We would all have a hover car and pop over to Mars for a pint of milk before getting the robot to do the house work. Well it didn't really turn out like that - unfortunately.

Whether you are a seasoned **Ufologist** [a professional who studies the UFO phenomenon for a living] or a complete newcomer to this subject I hope that everyone can get something out of this book. Even if you do not believe in the alien agenda, or in the existence of aliens, the aim of the book is to both entertain and to inform. Perhaps you will believe in aliens when you have read it!

Another thing to point out is that I am not driven to this subject because I have had a personal experience. I have never been abducted and have never seen an alien or a flying saucer. I do not have a tiny implant in my head placed there by aliens whilst out walking my dog, to my knowledge anyway. I would say that this puts me in a position of impartiality and more able to see the subject as a whole, rather than concentrating on one single experience which so many witnesses do.

I also am critical, cynical and do not believe in any other **paranormal** [unusual phenomena or experiences that lack an obvious scientific explanation] subjects. In fact I do not consider the UFO subject to be paranormal. I do not believe in ghosts, the after-life, the bible, astral projection or fairies and I am not religious. I do believe that there is a lot mankind has yet to find out about the Universe and how it works, and that the ultimate question has still to be answered: why is there a universe anyway? My background is scientific. I studied science 'A' levels at school then took a degree in Electrical and Electronic Engineering. This type of education teaches you, that in order to get to the truth, you must never make assumptions. As soon as you make an assumption, then any argument or analysis which follows from it is flawed. It teaches you that if assumptions are made then they must be clearly stated and referred back to. In my career as an Engineer working for Rolls Royce I remember one senior engineer had a saying that he used to repeat over and over again. "never make assumptions!", then he would write the word

ASS  U  ME

... and say, "Because it makes an ASS of U and an ASS of ME", pointing at the letters. This is very much my background. In order to believe something, I need good evidence. The UFO subject has had so many very good witnesses, that it is impossible to discard. If you want to learn more about those witnesses refer to the detailed write up which is given in the index.

Another important point to mention is something which **Stanton Friedman** [a highly respected scientist and Ufologist, **46**] often states is that most UFO incidents and sightings are probably not real and only some are. This is a problem which makes the subject easy for some people to debunk. What they do is pick on a UFO case which is clearly flawed then go into great detail as to why the incident makes no sense. They then conclude that all such cases must therefore be frauds. An item on the BBC news caught my eye recently, which discussed a reasonably convincing story of a woman describing a UFO hovering above her house. The reporter then went on to explain that many Ufologists also claim that **crop circles** [patterns created by the flattening of crops such as wheat, barley and rapeseed] are produced by UFOs. The BBC reporter interviewed an old man, whose hobby it is to make crop circles using a plank of wood. The article concluded with the reporter basically saying - yeah well she saw "something", but this old guy makes crop circles with a plank so UFOs must be made up too! How scientific is that? My point being that there are hoaxes, and there are liars and people do try to muddy the waters, but this in itself proves nothing.

I do not claim that all UFO stories are the truth, most are probably not. However, I am certain some are genuine and it only takes one to be true for the UFO case to be proven. If I was asked to give a single piece of evidence which proves that aliens and UFOs exist, it would be the **disclosure project** [an American pressure group whose purpose is to make the U.S. Government reveal secrets it keeps about UFOs, **24**] 2001 video. In this video many extremely reliable witnesses testify that they have seen UFOs and aliens.

Another hurdle that is often encountered when trying to argue the case is related to the previous point about dismissing the entire subject because of a single piece of fraudulent evidence. Deep within the human psyche is the ability, when faced with a fact that would completely change our reality, to deny that fact without a second thought regardless of its authenticity. It is a protection mechanism. In other words, our own psyche has the ability to protect us when threatened by something we distrust or threatens our accepted view of the world, like the ostrich burying its head in the sand. It is this characteristic which has helped the governments of the world cover up the alien presence for so

3

many years. The easiest person in the world to fool is yourself.

Having said all that, the book is not a scientific paper and therefore all of the statements and claims will not be backed up with meticulous evidence, although I have listed in the index and reference sections the main sources of my information. Some of the claims have been gleaned from the general UFO community.

It is now a commonly accepted view, especially in the UFO community, that the question is not "do aliens exist?", but "when will governments admit aliens exist?". If we look around us, there are already signs that governments and authorities are preparing us for some kind of disclosure. What are the signs? Previously classified documents in the UK are being drip-fed to the public. The documents are being released over a period of years. Why should they do it in this way? Why not just release them all at once? The reason is because governments know that eventually one day the entire truth will be revealed and the public need to be prepared. Each release of documents nudges the public gradually towards a state of mind where they are more likely to accept the truth.

There is always pressure on governments to let the truth out and in the day of the internet and modern communications, information is shared widely and governments are finding it harder to keep secrets. They know that the tide is turning and more people believe the mountain of evidence that is available. So you can see their predicament – they have kept the secret about aliens and UFOs for over 60 years and know that the masses are slowly learning the real truth. What do they do? One thing they are petrified of is just announcing it without any regard for the consequences. If they did this the public would be outraged that they had been lied to for so long, and would no longer trust them – revolution could ensue with possible unrest in the streets. Not only that, the public would no longer trust the entire system of government, because it is not just one administration that has kept the secret but many

4

governments, many prime ministers and many presidents. The entire democratic constitutions of the world would be brought into question. This is just one reason, among many others, why a government would not just announce the existence of aliens. So what they have done is construct a programme whereby the public are being gradually "warmed" to the idea that there may be aliens so as to soften the eventual blow. Part of this process is the releasing of files. Each release will then move the public closer to the view that aliens are a real possibility.

Other organisations have clearly been preparing their followers for disclosure. The Vatican announced recently that if extraterrestrials were discovered this would not contradict the Bible or fundamental Christian beliefs.

Here is a quote from Reverend Jose Gabriel Funes, a Jesuit who directs the Vatican Observatory,

> "Aliens could be out there, and believing that the Universe may contain extraterrestrial life does not contradict a faith in God."

> "How can we rule out that life may have developed elsewhere?"

> "Just as there is a multitude of creatures on Earth, there could be other beings, even intelligent ones, created by God. This does not contradict our faith, because we cannot put limits on God's creative freedom."

> "Just as we consider earthly creatures as 'a brother' and 'sister,' why should we not talk about an 'extraterrestrial brother'? It would still be part of creation."

The Vatican has its own observatory and has been very interested in cosmology and the outer space alien for decades. The last thing they want is their power base crumbling when the truth comes out, so they are making their position clear now in preparation for the disclosure.

It is possible that the US Administration elected in November 2008 will be Democratic. In the past Democratic Presidents such as Kennedy, Carter and Clinton have been more inclined to want to disclose the existence of aliens. Republican presidents, such as Eisenhower, Reagan, and the first President Bush have been involved in the cover up. Ironically it was a Democrat, Truman, who set up **MJ12** [a top secret group of U.S. government and military officials created in 1947, **20**] who were responsible for the UFO cover up and keeping the existence of aliens out of the public arena. This was arguably excusable at the time, having just come out of a World War and with tension building towards the Cold War. It is rumoured that over the last 60 years there have been moves by governments to work towards a full disclosure, but for one reason or another, the moves have always been stifled. In fact "Close Encounters of The Third Kind" and "ET" were the first films which showed aliens as friendly or benevolent beings. These films were made as part of a programme to warm the public to the idea of aliens in preparation for a disclosure. However, disclosure never took place and here we are today still waiting.

It is interesting to ponder how the U.S. government will manage the disclosure process and how much they will reveal. Whatever is revealed, if it is an admission that they have known for 60 years, then why would anyone believe what they are saying? When they do reveal anything, the barrage of questions that they will face will be unprecedented. Once they reveal something are we to then assume that all of the other rumors in the UFO community are true?

Perhaps governments will try and orchestrate some kind of visitation in cahoots with an alien race, then allow the press in to film the whole process and hope that people will forget about the cover up that has gone on for so long. This is where my money would be. I do not think governments will just announce the facts out of the blue. I think that it will be an event or some kind of happening which will catapult the start of the disclosure. Whether orchestrated or not, this will be the excuse they need to finally come clean. I am sure there are people working on this problem behind closed doors. How will they do it?

Once this has happened, whatever form it takes, it will be a turning point in the history of mankind. Everyone will remember where they were and what they were doing on that day. Nobody should underestimate the importance of such an event. It will make 9-11 look like a storm in a tea cup and will change our lives forever.

We can only speculate as to the changes that will occur after disclosure. I have considered in this book the possible changes that could happen and what information would be good to know to help deal with those changes. Some chapters of the book tackle the aliens themselves, what they look like, and what to expect of them. Other sections discuss the political and technological issues of a new world.

# 2. UFOs

Before I start I need to point out that this chapter is not about trying to persuade anyone that UFOs exist. If you want to be convinced read the index where witnesses and incidents are described in detail. This chapter is written on the assumption that the crafts do exist. In order to move things on and consider the future, we cannot sit around all day pondering about whether the evidence is strong enough or whether what somebody said was true or false. So we will state the assumption here, that UFOs exist, and move on to some very interesting ground.

In this chapter we will learn a little about UFOs and how they can be detected. If we consider the thousands of sightings that have been made over the years, and sightings go back centuries, the craft fall into two main categories. The first category is the large UFO, and when I say large I mean large. Many UFO sightings describe massive craft. Typical quotes from witnesses are, "bigger than a football pitch" or "a mile wide". Famous sightings of this type include the **Hudson Valley sightings** [1982 multiple witnesses see UFO north of New York City, **61**], the **Stephenville sightings** [2008 multiple witnesses see UFO in Texas, **62**], the **Illinois sightings** [2000 multiple witnesses see UFO, **63**], **Phoenix sightings** [1997 thousands witness this UFO, **64**]. The larger craft are often described as black triangles or 'V' shaped craft with lights along the sides. These craft are considered by many to be mother ships or "cities in the sky". The second category is the classic flying saucer shaped smaller UFO. Reported sightings are in the range from about 10 feet wide to 50 feet wide. Of the thousands of sightings, most are reported to be circular or disc shaped, some having a dome shape above the disc, similar to a bowler hat.

One problem with UFO sightings is that people rarely see extreme detail on the craft. They either describe a uniform shape or more often just coloured lights. They rarely report any detail such as windows, or external contour features such as doors, wings or exhaust gear. Almost always the craft have a very simple shape, such as a disc, cigar or triangle, or are described simply as glowing coloured lights. An explanation as to the reason for the simple shape and the coloured lights is given by **Bob Lazar** [a scientist who worked at a secret U.S. government facility on acquired UFOs, **40**]. In 1988-89 Lazar worked at S4, a secret government facility, where he alleges 9 alien flying discs are kept. The craft he saw are all of the second smaller variety, but all have or had slightly different shapes.

Bob actually witnessed a test flight of one of the UFO craft, saw it operate, went inside it and attempted to work out the operation of the whole thing. According to him, these craft exhibit a very intense electric field. The field is so intense that it causes air molecules (oxygen and nitrogen) to emit photons of light. This means that glowing light is seen around the craft almost like a halo. The electric field is a byproduct of the crafts advanced propulsion system, which we will explore later in the book. So in a similar way that a neon light glows when we apply electricity, air itself can glow different colours if subjected to a large enough electric field. This is why so many of the UFO sightings are described as a glowing light in the sky with no discernable detail. Colours that have been reported are red, green, blue, orange, white and yellow.

Today scientists have some understanding of the properties of strong electric or electromagnetic fields. One property is that the field can break down the air and cause a discharge like lightning, or a spark in an electric lighter. The higher the field, the more likely a discharge will occur. Breakdown and discharge usually occurs around corners and edges, anything that has a sharp corner, or anything that sticks out. This is the reason why the craft are very simple in their shape are smooth and have no edges to prevent electric discharge. According to Bob Lazar even the inside of the craft are like this. There are no sharp edges anywhere, even where the ceiling meets the floor. Bob Lazar quotes, "It's as if the whole thing is fashioned out of wax and then melted slightly so there are no sharp edges".

So we have evidence which suggests that a strong electric or electromagnetic field is emitted by a UFO craft. We know this because of the smoothness of the crafts themselves, the coloured lights, and Bob Lazars testimony. There have also been many strange electromagnetic effects reported during UFO sightings, such as cars spluttering to a halt due to electrical failure and magnetic compasses no longer functioning correctly. Later in this chapter we will discuss how it is possible to use these phenomena to design a device which can detect the presence of an intense electromagnetic field and hence warn us of the presence of a UFO. Perhaps one day this will save your life!

Before we discuss that, I have talked a little about the appearance and also the two broad groups of UFOs. Now I would like to touch on the actual way you might see them move, their dynamics, and how they stay off the ground.

Let's start by discussing flying. What is flying? Rather than consider flying, let's just consider "getting off the ground", because the two are not the same. There are three different ways we earthlings have discovered that will get us off the ground and into the sky. The first method is the hot air balloon. This method relies on the fact that the air around us is a fluid which has mass. If we create an object which is on average less dense, or lighter than the air surrounding it, then it will float above the surrounding air. The hot air balloon is essentially floating on the air in the same way a plastic duck floats in the bath. This first method of getting us off the ground is not really "flying" but floating. The second method is what we would consider flying. The Wright brothers achieved the first flight in 1903. The difference between this and a balloon is that the plane is heavier than air, whereas the balloon is not; hence the Wright brothers aeroplane was not floating, but flying. Flight is achieved by the craft creating pressure underneath the wings due to the airflow above and below the wing causing lift; this is also true of a helicopter. When a bird flaps its wings it creates this same effect. This is what we humans call flying. The third method that earthlings have discovered is used by a space rocket or indeed a fire work. The upward thrust uses Newton's third law. By creating force in a downward direction an equal and opposite thrust is created in an upward direction propelling the rocket. In this type of motion we would not consider the craft to be "flying". The first two methods discussed here would not work on the moon or on any planet that has no atmosphere, they rely totally on there being surrounding air to work. The third method would work without air, but requires lots of fuel to eject out the back of the craft in order to project it off the ground. Of the methods mankind has discovered, two don't work in space and the third requires lots of heavy fuel. Having considered these three methods you now need to forget them! The UFO doesn't "get off the ground" using any of these methods, and it certainly doesn't "fly", "float" or use "thrust" but it does "get off the ground", and I will now explain how.

We need to consider why things stay on the ground in the first place. We have all heard of gravity. In everyday physics we know that a very large object such as the Earth attracts all other objects and causes them to accelerate towards it. We observe this when an apple falls from a tree. This pulling force is dependant on the weight or mass of the large object. All objects on Earth are attracted to each other by gravity. The size of the force is so miniscule you do not notice the attraction between objects, only towards the Earth. It is only when something becomes as large as the Earth that there is a significant pull. We should now consider why a large mass pulls all other masses towards it?

Consider a trampoline. Put a very heavy object in the middle of it, such as a cannon ball. What effect would the cannon ball have on smaller objects placed on the trampoline? They would be attracted to the large object because the trampoline surface becomes distorted or bent due to the large weight of the cannon ball. This bending causes other smaller objects to accelerate towards it. Our

Earth is very similar to the cannon ball except the forces act in a 3 dimensional way, not just 2. The Earth bends the 3 dimensional space around it into another dimension. We cannot see nor conceive this dimension and objects are pulled towards the Earth from every direction. Objects accelerate towards the Earth because the space is distorted due to the Earths mass; this distortion is called a gravitational field.

Now that we understand gravity, or at least can describe the effects of gravity, I can now go on to explain how a UFO craft stays off the ground. If it was possible to generate our own local distortion or gravitational field so that it could oppose the Earths field, we would be able to cancel out the effects of Earth's gravity and objects would just hang in mid air, or mid space. This is how the UFO craft work. In our current or accepted understanding of physics, it is believed that the only way to generate a distortion and produce a gravitational field is by having a heavy object such as the Earth. However, if we now go back to Bob Lazar, who has examined a real working flying saucer, he claims that the craft <u>can</u> generate a gravitational field <u>without</u> the need to have a heavy object such as the Earth. Bob Lazar told us in 1989 that the UFO craft used a special heavy element as the source to generate this field, the heavy element being **Element 115** [a chemical element which is not found on Earth which has some fascinating properties, **04**]. This element is not found anywhere in our Solar System, but has been brought here from other parts of the galaxy by aliens. In one of his videos Lazar states that there is gravity locked within all matter which in special cases can extend beyond the outside of the **atom** [an atom is a tiny particle of which all matter is composed]. By using this very heavy element, Element 115, the gravity field can extend beyond the perimeter of the atom, and then be focused and pointed in a direction to oppose the Earth's field, thus cancelling out the Earth's gravity leaving the craft stationary in space as it would be in outer space. When sitting in this mode, anyone in the craft would be weightless, just as an astronaut is weightless in orbit around the Earth.

I will go into the actual operation of the gravity generator in the technology chapter. What we are more interested in here is describing how the craft moves. Having explained how the craft manages to stay off the ground, we can see that they do not "fly" at all, nor do they "float", their mode of operation is like nothing us earthlings have ever achieved. This brings us on to the next question which is how do they move? Again, according to Bob Lazar, the crafts move using the same gravity generation system. This time instead of generating just enough distortion to oppose the Earth's field, it produces a massive distortion in one specific direction which enables it to disappear within the blink of an eye. Again, the beings within the craft would still experience weightlessness throughout; they would not feel any acceleration. Imagine jumping off a cliff, when falling you are in fact weightless. If there were no air resistance you would feel weightless until you hit the ground. So the UFO has created its own field and just falls into it, like falling off a cliff. The difference being that the acceleration the UFO can produce is thousands of times more than would be achieved falling off a cliff on planet Earth. Another point to note is that when the craft disappear in this "fast" mode they do so at 90 degrees to the plane of the disc. So if the disc were hovering like a Frisbee parallel to the Earth, the craft would shoot off vertically upwards. There is a classic case where this was witnessed in 2006 at **O'Hare International Airport** [a famous UFO multiple witness sighting, **65**]. The craft cut a perfect circle in the clouds as it departed vertically upwards.

Now that we understand in very basic terms the UFO's propulsion method we can begin to build up a picture of their characteristic movements. They have a mode where they hang almost stationary in the air, simply opposing the Earth's gravity, possibly moving around slightly. This mode is a little unstable, a bit like a person balancing on a tight rope, making constant corrections all the time to stay in position. Then within the blink of an eye the craft can shoot off at incredible speed.

If we consider radar recordings of UFOs, of which there have been many, they all record objects moving at incredible speed. Some recordings are in excess of 18,000 miles per hour. The fastest plane that we earthlings have made can go nowhere near this speed. It can certainly not accelerate to that speed instantly from a dead start. A vast number of UFO sightings have reported smallish craft, fairly stationary, which just shoot off without a trace. As well as this sudden darting movement, craft have been reported as doing right angle or acute turns, that is to say, sudden changes in direction at incredible speeds. In a human designed aircraft, if you tried to achieve this kind of sudden change in direction the **G forces** [force experienced when an object accelerates] would kill everyone on the craft. It would be like flying into a brick wall. The UFO can achieve this kind of manoeuvre and the beings within the craft remain weightless. The sudden change in direction of the craft corresponds to the re-directing of the gravity generator to point in a different direction. A further point to note is that their operation is totally silent.

Having discussed the dynamics of the smaller UFO type craft, larger crafts movements have been reported to be different. They too are totally silent and probably stay in the air using the same gravity generation technology, but have been recorded moving at a range of different speeds. Sometimes as slow as 10 miles per hour, sometimes 60 miles per hour, and occasionally at very high speeds similar to the smaller disc UFO.

I mentioned earlier that these UFOs are very big indeed. Not only that, they have been confirmed on radar that they are in fact solid objects, in the order of a mile wide. If something registers on a radar system then it must be solid. These large craft have never been seen landing on the Earth, only sitting in the sky, so where do they go? Where are they kept?

In order to suggest a likely place I will explain a little bit about **Karl Wolf** [who was a Sergeant in the US Air Force]. Karl Wolf's job was involved with repairing photographic equipment. One particular job he was assigned to in 1965 took him to a **NASA [21]** photographic laboratory where images from the lunar orbiter were being received. The lunar orbiter is a space probe which had been orbiting the Moon, sending back detailed photographic images of the Moon back to Earth. One point here about the Moon, is that, from Earth, we can only ever see one side of it. This is due to the way the Moon rotates always presenting the same face towards the Earth.

Here is a quote from Karl Wolf about his visit to the lab in 1965. Remember man did not make it to the Moon until 1969.

"I was interested in how the whole process functioned, how the data got from the lunar orbiter to the laboratory, I asked the young man if he'd describe the process to me, he did. About thirty minutes into the process he said to me, in a very distressed way, 'by the way we have discovered a base on the back side of the moon'. And then he proceeded to put photographs down in front of me and clearly in these photographs were structures, mushroom shaped buildings, spherical buildings and towers. And at that point I was very concerned because I knew we were working in compartmentalised security. He had breached security and I was actually frightened at that moment and I did not question him any further. And a few moments later someone did come into the room. I worked there for three more days and I remember going home and naively thinking I can't wait to hear about this on the evening news, and here it is more than thirty years later and I hope we hear about it tonight and I will testify under oath before congress."

Further, when **Neil Armstrong** [the first human to walk on the moon] did eventually go to the Moon in 1969 on the Apollo 11 mission NASA's broadcasts where picked up by **radio hams** [amateur radio enthusiast on the Earth]. The following exchange was picked up,

**NASA**: What's there?  Mission Control calling Apollo 11 ...

**Apollo** : These babies are huge, Sir! Enormous! OH MY GOD!  You wouldn't believe it!  I'm telling you there are other spacecraft out there, lined up on the far side of the crater edge! They're on the Moon watching us!

Then in 1979, **Maurice Chatelin** [former chief of NASA Communications Systems] confirmed that Neil Armstrong had indeed reported seeing two UFOs on the rim of a crater.

After returning to Earth Neil Armstrong did not speak to the media until 2005.  Many think that the reason why he never spoke to the media was because he had been warned by NASA not to talk publicly of the UFOs he witnessed. Armstrong did not want to lie to the public and so chose to not speak to the media at all.  Having considered the last two pieces of evidence, I hope I have illustrated clearly where these massive motherships are probably kept: on the backside of the Moon!

Now that I have given details of the size, shape, appearance, movement and where they are kept, we will go back to how to detect one.  Other than visual detection with our own eyes, we can build a device that will detect the UFOs large electromagnetic field.

Before I go into the ins and outs of such a device I need to point out why you might need to detect one.  There are two basic reasons:  the first would be to enable you to gather more evidence to prove their existence.  The second, which might help us in the future, is to create a kind of early warning system to let us know aliens are coming, so that we can then take appropriate action.

Devices which detect the presence of a magnetic field are commonly called magnetometers. A sophisticated magnetometer would be able to measure the field in different ways, such as the strength, the frequency [which is the speed of vibration], and the direction in which it is acting. It would then be able to give a plot or printout of these characteristics over the time period of the sighting.

If we were to combine this technology with technology similar to a radar system, it would be possible, by adding some electronics and software along with a visual display of some kind, to have a hand held UFO detector that would show on a screen the position of the UFO and its height in relation to us. The device would be able to differentiate between normal aircraft and UFOs by measuring its magnetic effects. Maybe one day we will all carry one in our pocket.

Needless to say this type of device is not yet available to buy and a sophisticated magnetometer is very expensive. It is possible however, to make simpler versions of this device using components we could buy from a local hardware store. The first design uses a simple magnet suspended by a string and buzzer to warn of any magnetic disturbance. The second is a more sophisticated design and relies on an electronic compass to detect irregularities in our surrounding magnetic field.

Details are given below,

### Magnet on a String UFO Detector

This device is very simple [see diagram overleaf]. You will need a small solid conducting ring, about 2cm in diameter, perhaps a metal washer. You also need a small rectangular shaped magnet. Using a thin, 50cm long, piece of conducting wire with no insulation, attach the magnet to the end of the wire. Suspend the magnet so that the wire passes through the metal hole. Fix the top of the wire and the washer using a non conducting structure, such as a wooden frame. Next connect a battery and an alarm to the washer and to the top of the wire so that if the magnet moves or sways causing the wire to touch the washer, a circuit is made, thus setting off the alarm; simple!

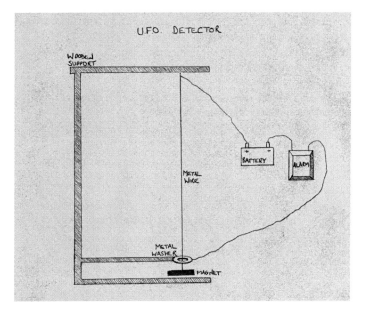

Clearly there are drawbacks with this design. It is large and cumbersome. It is susceptible to wind and vibration and can only work on a flat surface. Having said all of that, I would recommend installing it in your loft employing a really loud alarm, and perhaps wire the alarm to the mains instead of a battery. By placing it in the loft the device is not likely to be bumped by passing toddlers or pets. If you make the washer smaller, then the device will be more sensitive. Imagine your family's reaction if it goes off one day. You could all rush out into the street and look up at the skies for a flying saucer, then get vaporized into thin air by an alien death ray.

Alternatively rush inside the house and hide under the floorboards. I will deal with hiding under the floorboards later in the chapter on protection.

**Electronic UFO Detector**

For those with a flare for electronics, a more sensitive and compact UFO detector can be made using an electronic compass and a small micro controller. The detector runs on a 9 volt battery and sets off a flashing light and alarm when there are magnetic field irregularities.

Details of how to build the detector can be found at the Images Scientific Instruments website, http://www.imagesco.com/kits/ufo-detector-kit.html.

# 3. Aliens

If you were thinking that there has been contact here on Earth with a race of aliens you would be very much mistaken. There has been contact with many races of alien! The claims vary on the number of known races of outerspace alien that have passed our way. **Phil Schneider** [a government engineer and geologist, who confronted aliens in 1979, **41**] claimed that there are 11 distinct types of alien, but **Clifford Stone** [a U.S. Army Sergeant , **44**] beats that claim with 57 types! Clifford Stone, a very reliable witness claims that there is a secret Government publication entitled, "The EBE [Extraterrestrial Biological Entity] Guidebook" which describes the physiological characteristics of 57 types of EBE. In this Guidebook, detailed information is given on all the known types of alien. This suggests that behind closed doors the Government has extensive information that has been gathered presumably directly from aliens and from **UFO crash retrievals** [incidents where a UFO crashes and wreckage is recovered and examined]. What I will describe in this chapter is an outline of the information that has leaked out about what is known of these aliens.

I will sometimes refer to "the shadow government", and will briefly explain what I mean by this. It is believed that in 1947, President Harry Truman set up MJ12, a secret group of military and intelligence officials, specifically to control activities relating to UFOs and aliens. This group, or indeed other similar groups which may now be in place, have become detached from or perhaps not answerable to the U.S. Government. They are said to operate outside of the normal U.S. Government processes, and that nobody, including several past presidents, have control over these groups. This is what I mean by "shadow government".

Some further background information is necessary before we talk about the creatures themselves. It is an accepted view within the UFO community that a secret underground base exists at Dulce, New Mexico, a large, sparsely-populated baron area of land. The base is rumoured to be two and half miles deep and comprises seven levels. The lower levels are occupied by various races of aliens, which are described later in this chapter. I need to point out that this base is not just made up of a few large rooms. It is rumoured to be many square miles in size, and there are thousands of beings residing there. When I refer to the Dulce base, I am referring to an entire civilization living deep below the earth. There are rumoured to be many more bases, probably smaller than Dulce throughout the world, but we will come on to that later in the book.

The information in this chapter comes from whistleblowers and witnesses who have previously held positions which gave them direct access to aliens and alien technology. Over the years many witnesses have spoken about the existence of alien beings on Earth, or perhaps a better phrase would be "beneath the Earth". Some of the witnesses are listed below. This is not a complete list, but the names given here are some of the main witnesses.

**Phil Schneider** [41], A geologist and structural engineer employed in building underground bases.

**Robert Collins** [42], Ex US Air Force who specialised in many different technologies.

**Clifford Stone** [44], Retired Sergeant in the US Army.

**Thomas Castello** [45], Ex security guard & CCTV technician at the Dulce underground base.

**Bob Dean** [47], Army Sergeant Major.

You can look up information on these people in the index.

In the descriptions which follow I have tried to use information that is generally consistent with many witnesses testimony rather than rely on one or two witnesses. I could go into great detail as to what each witness has said, but this would require another book. Instead I have extracted useful information which describes the aliens themselves, their appearance, their character, their eating habits and whether you could invite one round for tea to meet your mother. At some point in the future it may be the case that we need to interact with some of them on a daily basis, so it would be very useful to know in advance what to expect.

In the descriptions which follow, don't worry if you do not recognise the places where the aliens come from as I will explain these places in detail later in the book.

# The Small Gray

## Where do they come from?

Zeta Reticulum and Bellatrix in Orion

## Are there different types?

There are known to be three slightly different types, each having different finger arrangements. Two of the types are from Zeta Reticulum and a slightly shorter race from Bellatrix. These are sometimes called Brown or Orange Grays. All are from the same root race.

## What do they look like?

As you would expect they are small and gray, between 3 to 5 five feet tall. They are erect standing **bipeds** [which means they walk on two legs] with a very large head containing two brains. Their heads are larger than a human's head with no hair, eyebrows or eye lashes. They have large opaque black almond shaped eyes, which are slanted at approximately 30 degrees, and have vertically slit pupils. Their eyes are described as being very creepy and make a lasting impression on people who have see them. Their heads are domed and look similar in shape to a human fetus head. They have spindly arms and legs and a thin torso, slightly resembling a praying mantis. Their long hands reach down to their knees when standing with their arms by their sides, and a small palm leads to claw like spindly fingers. Normally they have two short and two long fingers, but some only have three fingers. Their skin is slightly reptilian in texture, grey in colour and tough. Small feet with four small claw-like toes complete this insect like creature. Internally they have a non-functioning digestive system, waste products being secreted through the skin.

Artists Impression – The Small Gray

## How do they behave?

They are extremely logical beings and have a love of technology. Religious activity annoys them. Any activity which does not have an obvious logical context confuses them, which means they have no sense of humour and do not understand poetry. Their movements are very slow, deliberate and precise. Although they have high intelligence, they take a long time to make decisions. They are believed to possess a telepathic ability, which as a group gives them a collective consciousness.

## What are they up to?

Some types of Small Gray work for the **Draconian Reptilian aliens** [another race of aliens described later in this chapter] at the Dulce Base and are subservient to them. At this base, the Small Gray aliens are involved in several unpleasant activities. They abduct humans, for genetic experiments and mind programming. They use implants to monitor humans; attempts by humans to remove these implants have sometimes resulted in the death of the human. After many years of practice and research, they have become experts in the manipulation of both the human body and mind. One of their projects at Dulce is to create a new type of being, the human-gray hybrid.

It is the Small Gray alien that has been recovered from UFO crashes such as **Roswell** [a famous UFO crash in 1947 in which aliens were recovered, **66**] and **Missouri** [another UFO crash which occurred in 1941]. Three Small Gray aliens are believed to have lived in captivity with the U.S. military on separate occasions between 1947 and 1993. The first of these aliens was the only survivor of the 1947 Roswell UFO crash.

## What do they eat?

Blood and other biological fluids is the mainstay of the Small Gray's diet. They abduct human beings and certain animals, usually cattle, to make these fluids. The formula they produce includes **amniotic water** [this is the nourishing and protecting liquid contained within the womb of a pregnant woman], **blood plasma** [the liquid component of

26

blood in which blood cells are suspended and which contains dissolved proteins, glucose, mineral ions, hormones and carbon dioxide] and several other soft tissue body parts which are raw, usually **bovine** [from a cow or bull]. The Gray's requirement for bovine innards explains the thousands of **mutilated cattle [60]** which are found all over the world. The mixture is a nearly-clear mixture with the texture of pureed peaches. They try not to consume this substance around humans, because the odour is totally obnoxious to us. They can spend days or even weeks between feedings.

Blood plasma and amniotic fluid are the two most vital ingredients for their diet. The 'sap' of some parasitic plants can keep these beings alive for months. Red grapes and okra plants can also be added to their formula to keep them alive if they do not have the plasma and amniotic formula.

Another chilling part of their diet is a substance which is generated by the human brain when we are under stress or in fear of our lives. Phil Schneider claims they consume this substance like a recreational drug as a human would use cocaine. The substance may well be a hormone, and is sometimes known as "life energy" or "soul energy". Incidentally other types of alien, such as the Reptilian also have a liking for this "drug".

**Would you invite them to meet your mother?**

Definitely not, bearing in mind that the Small Gray is quite happy to extract your soft tissue organs and all of your blood, and then liquidize this into a protein drink for its afternoon refreshment. They can also exercise mind control and they stink.

# The Large Gray

## Where do they come from?

A red star named Betelgeuse in the Orion constellation

## Are there different types?

Not known.

## What do they look like?

As you would expect they are large and gray, between 6 to 8 feet tall. Their height is often exaggerated by humans when describing them. They are erect standing bipeds and generally look similar to the Small Gray. Their heads are large with no hair, eyebrows or eyelashes. Their skin is extremely pale in colour almost white. It is possible that this race is actually a hybrid of the Short Gray and a taller race. The nose is much larger than that of a Small Gray.

## How do they behave?

They have similar characteristics of the Small Grays, are less vicious towards humans but still considered hostile.

## What are they up to?

The Large Grays have an overseeing role over the Small Grays. They are known to have carried out diplomatic activities and missions, such as negotiating treaties. It is the Large Gray species which met with President Eisenhower in 1954 and formed the Greada Treaty. This Treaty gave the Grays permission to abduct cattle in exchange for technology given to us by them. It is also believed to be this race which met with representatives of the U.S. Government in 1971 at Hollomon Air Force Base. They share the same interests as the Small Gray in areas such as genetic experiments and mind control.

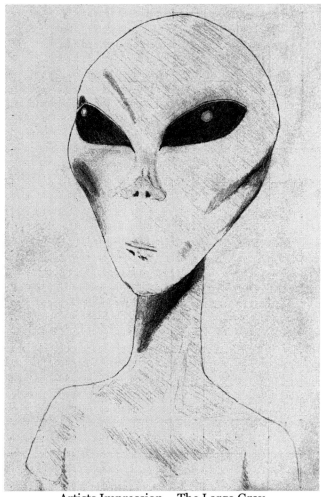

Artists Impression – The Large Gray

**What do they eat?**

They presumably have a similar diet to the Small Gray.

**Would you invite them to meet your mother?**

No.  The very sight of a Tall Gray would probably give your mother a heart attack.   They also smell very bad and have been known to attack humans with a radioactive blue beam.

# The Indigenous Reptilian

## Where do they come from?

Earth!, yes Earth. An ancient extraterrestrial race of Reptilians inhabited the Earth many years before man and played a role in the creation of humanity.

## Are there different types?

There are two types: the 'Ruling Caste' and the 'Worker Caste'.

## What do they look like?

The Reptilian stands between 7 to 8 feet tall and as expected has the look of a reptile. They too are erect standing bipeds. The Ruling Caste is grayish-white in colour and the Working Caste is greenish-brown.

The head is slightly conical in shape and has two bony ridges riding from the brow, across a back sloping skull. There appears to be no bridge between their eyes. The nasal openings are at the end of a small, flattened nose and are described as two small slits that slant upwards in a V formation. Small openings can be seen on the side of their heads, but no ears as such. The eyes contain vertically slit pupils, with a flame or an orange coloured surround. They have wide lipless mouths which contain various types of teeth, including fangs. Some have thin, fleshy spines under their chin.

Their skin is scaled, usually greenish brown or light grey in colour, and hairless. The scales on their backs, thighs and upper arms are quite large, with hands, abdomen and face being covered with smaller scales, allowing more flexibility.

Reptilian's bodies are lean and firm with powerful arms and legs, long arms and 3 fairly long fingers and an opposable thumb. The feet have 3 toes and one recessed fourth toe that is toward the back side of the ankle. Claws on

31

the hands and feet are short and blunt. They do not have teats on their upper torso and there is no navel.

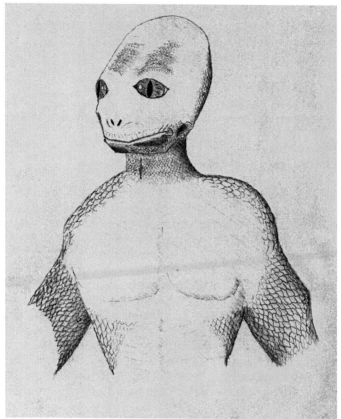

Artists Impression - Indigenous Reptilian

Reptilian beings can be both tailed and tailless. The tails differ in size and are held off the ground. Their posterior can be either human-like, with a vertical slit shielding an excretory orifice, or it can be a rounded muscular area extending from the base of the spine to the upper thigh region. Genitalia are concealed within a vertical slit located at the base of the torso.

## How do they behave?

The Ruling Caste Indigenous Reptilian race consider themselves to be genuine natives of the Earth and human beings to be squatters. A group of Reptilians is known as a Hive and the race is absolutely void of any care, concern or compassion for human beings. The Worker Caste can be friendly, as long as they are allowed to speak first. They will answer if you address them, are very cautious beings, and consider most humans to be hostile. They usually seem surprised when they find many humans are open and trustworthy. The Working Caste is generally used for physical labour and they have a no-nonsense get-back-to-work attitude. They have a different attitude to time than humans. It is not important to them in the way it is to us.

## What are they up to?

At the Dulce Base, the Worker Caste does daily chores including mopping the latex floors, cleaning cages, bringing food to hungry people and other species. It is their job to formulate the proper food mixture for various species that have been created by the **Draco Race** [described next].

## What do they eat?

Meat, insects and a large variety of plants including vegetables and fruit. They prefer their meat raw and very fresh, but have learned to enjoy some cooked meat like rare beef steak. Unlike the Grays, they eat frequently and usually carry or send for food during their breaks. The Ruling Caste is very secretive about their food preferring to eat in private. They enjoy much of the same food that humans do, and are often seen secretly munching on a freshly found snail.

## Would you invite them to meet your mother?

You could possibly invite a Worker Caste home for tea only if you had established some trust with it first. This would involve being totally subservient and only speaking when spoken to. You would need to warn your mother of the guest's appearance in advance, that is, a 7 foot tall lizard, and then ensure that she understood not to speak first.

# The Draconian Reptilian

## Where do they come from?

Alpha Draconis star system

## Are there different types?

There are two main types, the Ciakar and the Warrior Caste.

## What do they look like?

The Ciaker Draco is considered to be the royal line of Draco Reptilian race and range from 14 to 22 feet in height and can weigh up to 1,800 pounds! They have winged appendages and are described as awesome and look remarkably like a dragon.

The Warrior Caste Draco is a 7 to 8 foot tall biped, and is feared throughout the galaxy for its fighting ability. It has vertically slit pupils and skin similar to that found on the stomach of a lizard.

Dracos are not seen as often as other Reptilian aliens. They are similar in appearance to indigenous Reptilians, but do have distinct physical differences. The Draco has wings, whereas the indigenous Reptilians do not. The wings consist of long, thin bony spines or ribs that protrude out from the back. The ribs are adjoined by flaps of leathery dark skin. Normally wings are kept in a retracted position. Another physical difference to the indigenous Reptilian is that some Dracos have horns. They are located and develop midway between the brow and the top of the skull. Horns are conical in shape and have blunt tips. The Draco Reptilian has a much more athletic build than other Reptilian beings. Their upper torsos are extremely lean and their neck muscles splay out from the base of their jaw to their shoulder blades.

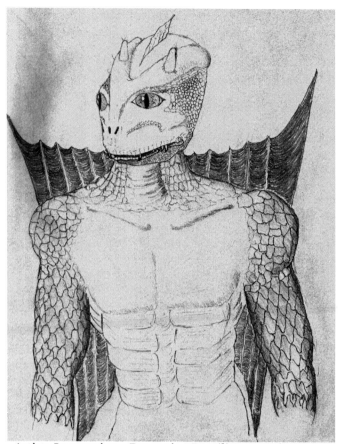
Artists Impression - Draconian Reptilian, Warrior Caste

**How do they behave?**

They are extremely intelligent, clairvoyant and can be very sinister. According to the Draconian world view, they were the first intelligent species in the galaxy and seeded many worlds with their biological off-spring. They therefore see themselves as the natural rulers of all Reptilian controlled worlds such as the Earth, and view humans as an inferior species.

**What are they up to?**

These aliens are in command of the Earth based Reptilians. The Earth based Reptilians (indigenous Reptilian) are in turn in command of the Large Grays, who are in command of the Small Grays.

The Dracos are interested in harvesting the Earth's resources and ensuring that these resources are efficiently exploited.

It is rumoured that the Draco Reptilian species are involved in controlling human beings who hold high office and therefore controlling institutions and financial systems.

**What do they eat?**

Their diet is similar to the indigenous Reptilian which includes lots of raw fresh meat.

**Would you invite them to meet your mother?**

No, the Ciaker type would not fit inside your house. The warrior caste has the strength of 10 men and could kill you in the blink of an eye.

## The Sirian

**Where do they come from?**

Sirius B star system

**Are there different types?**

They vary in skin colour.

**What do they look like?**

Very human-like erect standing bipeds, but with a slightly Reptilian look about them. They vary in skin colours, some are red, some beige and some black. They have a very high forehead which is almost cone like. The planets around Sirius B are occupied by reptilian and aquatic-type beings.

**How do they behave?**

Their society is more motivated by political thought patterns and they are not religious.

**What are they up to?**

The Sirians are believed to have played a role in providing exotic technology such as time/inter-dimensional travel to shadow government agencies involved in both the Philadelphia experiment and the Montauk project [secret U.S. Government projects involved with time-visual-shielding (making things invisible) and brain-washing]. They are supposed to have had a role in technology exchanges to help the U.S. develop a military capability against future alien threats. The assistance involved biological weapons research and it is claimed that the Ebola virus was given to the government by the Sirians. These beings are believed to have access to some sort of time travel which allows access to key points in time.

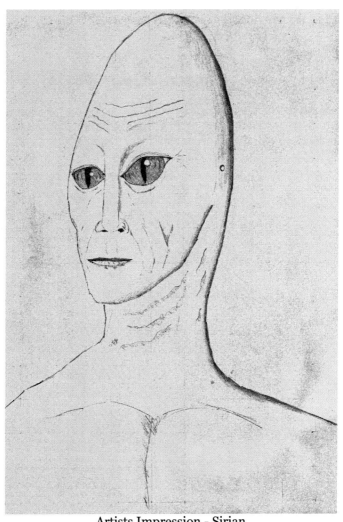

Artists Impression - Sirian

**What do they eat?**

Not known.

**Would you invite them to meet your mother?**

Possibly. Their appearance would probably be acceptable
and they are rumoured to have had communication with
humans in the past, namely with shadow government
officials.

# The Anunnaki

## Where do they come from?

Nibiru, which is within our solar system in a highly elliptical orbit.

## Are there different types?

Not known.

## What do they look like?

Very large, 6 to 8 feet, possibly 9 feet tall and human in appearance. Anunnaki are rumoured to be a cross between the aliens of Sirius B and a race from Orion. The cross breeding occurred hundreds of thousands of years ago.

## How do they behave?

They are religious but this does not necessarily mean they are benevolent. They have been known to be violent.

## What are they up to?

They periodically return to the Earth to determine how effectively Earth's resources have been utilised by humanity and by those extraterrestrial races playing a role in managing humanity. The Anunnaki visited Earth around 300,000 years ago and allegedly helped to create man by interfering with the evolution of an ancient version of man. They did this in order to create a race of slaves (the human race) in order to carry out mining activities on Earth. This information ties in with Bob Lazars claims, that he read briefing documents stating that man was a product of externally corrected evolution and that man as a species had been genetically altered 65 times. The Annunaki is said to have an overseeing relationship with the Reptilians who currently control the Earth, although it is not known what the extent of this relationship is. The Anunnaki are involved in influencing long term human evolution through elite groups, systems and institutions, and by influencing human consciousness. They may be in competition with the Draco Reptilian for control of Earth.

Artists Impression - Anunnaki

**What do they eat?**

They are carnivorous.

**Would you invite them to meet your mother?**

Possibly. They are human in appearance, but very tall. There is not much known about how violent they may be. They allegedly met with the ancient Sumerian people on Earth thousands of years ago, who considered them to be Gods.

## The Nordic or Aryan

### Where do they come from?

Pleiades star cluster in the constellation of Taurus.

### Are there different types?

Not known.

### What do they look like?

They are human looking and are so named because they resemble Nordic, Scandinavian, or Aryan racial images. Their hair is blond, and eyes are blue. They are tall, most guess at 11 to 13 feet tall, statuesque, and attractive.

### How do they behave?

Nordics will not break the so called universal law of non interference [06]. This is a law which is known about throughout our Galaxy which states that different races should not interfere with each other in any way, whether to benefit them or otherwise. They have a high regard for life.

### What are they up to?

They choose primarily to just observe. Perhaps their motives are to create a harmony between the different creeds of the Galaxy.

### What do they eat?

One thing is certain; they do not eat other races of aliens.

## Would you invite them to meet your mother?

Yes, absolutely. They are polite and they don't interfere with human affairs.

Artists Impression – Nordic or Aryan

If we count all of the types of alien I have described here including variations, the total is 11 different species. There are known to be many other types in addition to the ones described, some of which are hybrids, including human hybrids. Bear in mind that the information given here could just be a fraction of what is known by the shadow government.

It is incredible that such Earth shattering information can be kept secret. I will discuss the political implications of this and the reasons why it is covered up in the politics chapter. But first of all we might need to know how to deal with one of these entities should we bump into one in a dark alley.

# 4. Alien Encounter

The first thing to bear in mind is that if you ever meet an alien, nothing can really prepare you for the sense of fear and uncertainty that you would feel. It's not the same as meeting an aggressive unpleasant person down the pub who has decided to take an instant dislike to you. Imagine being confronted by a wild hungry lion, except the lion is more intelligent than you, can read your mind and sense your emotions. Now we're getting a little closer to the feeling. People who say that we should just immediately assume aliens are friendly for the benefit of intergalactic relations are very commendable, but I cannot believe these people would feel this way if they were to actually encounter one.

You might be thinking that this would never happen to you. I am not saying it definitely would. What I am saying is that there are a number of species of alien, some of which I have described earlier, that are living on this planet. Most are not particularly pleasant. I am also saying that their agenda will become known to the public at large at some point in the future and that the Earth might become a very different place. I can't say it is definitely going to happen, but it might. Wouldn't it be useful to know what to do under the circumstances, just in case?

Here's what you do: simply look up at the sky pointing at a cloud and shout, "Look out here comes your mother". Then run for your life as fast as you can... I am of course joking. I couldn't resist a bit of harmless light relief. Seriously, there is no harm in considering what you should do, because the actions I just described would probably get you killed or at least knocked out for a few hours.

Not a great deal is known about the weapons that aliens might carry. However, there are two witnesses who have given accounts of weapons used by aliens. Thomas Castello, who purportedly worked at the Dulce Base as a security guard, describes in detail a device known as a flash gun. This is how he describes it,

"It is an advanced beam weapon that can operate on three different phases. Phase one, like Star Trek, can stun and maybe kill, if the person has a weak heart. On phase two, it can levitate anything, no matter what it weighs. Phase three is the serious business mode. It can be used to paralyze anything that lives; animal, human, alien and plant. On the higher position on the same mode, it can create a temporary death. I assure you, any doctor would certify that person is dead, but their life essence lingers in some strange limbo, some kind of terrible state of non-death. In 1 to 5 hours the person will revive, slowly; first the bodily functions will begin, and in a few minutes, consciousness followed with full awareness. In that mode the alien scientists re-programme the human brain and plant false information. When the person awakes, he 'recalls' the false information as information he gained through life experience.

There is no way for a person to learn the truth. The human mind 'remembers' and believes completely the false data. If you attempt to inform them, they would laugh or get angry. They never believe the truth. Their mind always forgets the experience of re-programming. You asked if the flash gun is difficult to operate. A two year old child could use it with one hand. It resembles a flash light, with black glass conical inverted lens. On the side are recessed knobs in 3 curved grooves. Each knob is sized differently. The closer the knob to the hand, the less the strength. It's that simple. Each knob has 3 strengths also, with automatic stops at each position. The strongest position will vaporize any thing that lives. That mode is so powerful it will leave no trace of what it vapourised.

Everybody calls them Flash Guns, or more commonly "the Flash" or "my Flash" when talking about it. In the manual it is first introduced as the Armolux Weapon. After that, it is explained as the Flash Gun."

My advice is, if they get what appears to be a flashlight out of their pocket, you need to act quickly and take cover. It is possible that all aliens residing at Dulce, that is both types of Gray and both types of Reptilian, carry these weapons.

Castello goes on to describe another type of weapon they sometimes employ; he is referring to the Dulce Base in this next statement,

"The weapon, besides the Flash Gun, mostly used is a form of sonic. Built in with each light fixture [and most camcorders] is a device that could render a man unconscious in seconds with nothing more than a silent tone."

Another witness who describes being hit by an alien weapon is Phil Schneider. His experience was quite different to the flash gun. He describes his attacker as "A 7 foot tall alien Gray". Whom, at close range, "just kind of waved his arm across his chest, then a blue beam hit me and opened me up like a fish." This almost knocked Schneider unconscious, luckily he was saved by a soldier who dragged him out of harms way, and the soldier was then killed soon after. Schneider survived the attack but was diagnosed with Cancer which he says was caused by radiation contained in blue beam. Schneider survived 15 years after this incident until he was murdered by the shadow government for telling his story to the American people.

So there we have it. A weapon which is unleashed simply by the wave of an arm; very nasty. I will now discuss individual types of alien and by considering what is known about them, the course of action you might take if you were to encounter one. I would recommend that, when reading the following pages you refer back to the alien description section to remind yourself of the individual alien characteristics.

## THE GRAY

Here is another quote from Thomas Castello on how you might deal with a Gray alien,

> "The Grays are photosensitive; any bright light hurts their eyes. They avoid sunlight and travel at night. Camera flashes cause them to back up. It could be used as a weapon against them, but they recover quickly. It could buy enough time to escape. Use commands, or nonsensical words in the form of commands and they will back up. Their brain is more logical than ours and they do not create fun. They do not understand poetry either. What really confuses them is saying things in pig latin. We learned that in a hurry, and used it against them [the Grays] in the **Dulce Wars** [a conflict which took place between aliens and humans at the Dulce Base]."

My advice is to invest in an extremely powerful flashlight, then surround the light with a ring of laser pens. You can buy laser pens from your local retailer. Wire all the pens and the flashlight to the same power source connected through a single on/off switch and use this weapon to shine in their eyes. Another idea would be to use a disco strobe light wired to a large battery such as a car battery. With regards to shouting out illogical commands, there is one possible problem here. The common alien language spoken at the Dulce Base is known as Eusshu, which is logical and easy to learn. However, I am not sure if there are any Eushhu phrase books on the shelves of WH Smiths. Nevertheless it is rumoured that most aliens residing on Earth can speak many different languages.

Bear in mind that the Grays are able to read your intent. According to Castello the human race broadcasts a frequency that the Grays can pick up. Each person has a slightly different frequency and that difference is what we would call a personality. When a human thinks, they broadcast strong impulses, in the case of fear the frequency is loud and easy to recognise, similarly, a calm and composed mind-set is far more difficult to recognise. Hence, another key piece of advice when faced with a Gray alien is to try and keep calm, and empty your mind. This probably sounds impossible under the circumstances, but these are the facts.

Here is another quote from Castello on controlling our thoughts,

"We can shield ourselves against them, however 95% of the human race never try to control their thoughts, and controlling our own thoughts is the best weapon. The average person rarely thinks in a clear pattern. That allows the brain to think in a chaotic way. Control your thoughts, and you can stop the aliens attempting to abduct and control you. Controlling my own thoughts has kept me alive for years."

**THE REPTILIAN**

Some Reptilians are soldiers employed to guard entrances to certain bases such as Dulce. The entrances are hidden and extremely remote so would not normally be encountered by humans. Thomas Castello describes here the rules you should follow when faced with a Reptilian alien. I am not sure which type of Reptilian he is referring to, probably the Draco Warrier,

"They choose to try to hide and avoid contact. They are soldiers, doing a job and usually there are 2 or 3 at each job site. They are 'manning' a remote post. They are not to bother the humans unless they are endangering the post. Most of them are not hostile and won't kidnap you, they may blast you with a flash gun that may paralyse you. You won't remember the flash for an hour or 2 and it can cause confusion and mild fear. It could cause you to black out (pass out) for a while. It is their way to escape and buy time to hide any visible equipment."

"They are fearsome to meet face to face, and their voices are harsh and whispery with heavy s's, but most of them understand English and several other languages. Wear something with a reptile (not something violent, like St. George killing the Dragon!) in sight. If you see one, keep your hands open, palm forward, arms down. That is the non-aggression approach. Don't raise your arms, unless told to. Don't carry anything in your hands or arms. If he doesn't run, walk slowly towards him. Let him speak first. They consider humans repulsive and hostile and threatening (with good reason!). Don't try to offer him anything, Don't touch him or anything of his. If he hisses at you, back up a couple feet, but don't look away! It simply means he finds you smelly. Don't try to overpower him, he is stronger than 10 or 12 men! Usually, if he hasn't run so far, he is curious and wants to talk to you. Fight your fear and your thoughts of panic."

So there we have it, some very good advice. The approach you might take is very different depending on the type of alien you are confronted with. I would recommend wearing a T-Shirt on which is printed a picture of a large **Komodo Dragon**! [a very large reptile native to Earth]. This, bizarre as it might sound, would encourage the Reptilian to trust you or at least be less hostile than he otherwise would.

Further testimony which may be of use is given by Phil Schneider, "They are mortal and they do die". He killed 2 large Grays with a pistol. An everyday firearm would definitely be useful, but bear in mind that the alien is likely to have a more advanced weapon, whatever that may be.

## OTHER ALIEN TYPES

There are friendlier aliens, which I touched on earlier. These are the Nordics, or Aryan beings, human in appearance, extremely tall with blonde hair and blue eyes. They do not break the **universal law** [which concerns the non-intervention with other intelligent life forms, **o6**].

Information given here is just a fraction of what is known behind our shadow government's doors. Surely we have a right to know the rest? Probably the best advice when encountering an alien would be to try and avoid it in the first place. This may sound obvious, but the best way to survive if the worst happens and aliens start to openly control our world, might be to hide. Think of people in World War Two who survived the Nazis by hiding in their loft or cellar. In the survival chapter, I will outline some key information which might be handy to know if that day arrived.

One question which a lot of people ask once they learn what the alien races are like is this: If the aliens all evolved on different worlds, then how come they all have a head with 2 eyes and a mouth, 2 hands and walk on 2 legs? Surely they would be mind bogglingly different to us and to each other? Why are they so similar? Some people then go on to use this fact as proof that the existence of aliens must be made up. The fact is they <u>are</u> similar in many ways and the fact that they are not mind bogglingly different does not prove anything. There is no generally accepted theory as to why we are so similar to alien species. This has yet to be explained, and is one of the great mysteries of the subject. A possible reason is that the planets where different alien species evolved were not always isolated from each other. The evolution of species on different planets has a common thread in the dim and distant past. Perhaps there has been some intelligence behind the spread of our evolution, throughout our galaxy?

# 5. Alien Abduction

There are many people who claim to have been abducted by aliens and then returned safely to Earth. I believe there may be many people who have been abducted by aliens that have not been returned safely to Earth. I come to this tentative conclusion by considering the missing person statistics in America.

In the United States alone, about 830,000 people are reported missing every year and entered into the FBIs Missing Persons Register. About 70% of these turn up within one week of going missing. However about 6% remain missing for over one year. If we consider that most of these people are probably permanently missing, that's about 50,000 per year, or 140 every day! These statistics are just the officially recorded cases and the actual number is probably much higher. Perhaps these people have committed suicide and their bodies have not been found. In America the total number of suicides per year is about 33,000 or 90 per day. Maybe they were murdered and their bodies hidden; in the U.S. about 17,000 people are murdered every year, about 46 per day. Bearing in mind these figures for actual suicide and homicide, I do not think that a number as high as 50,000 per year could be put down to these factors. I am not suggesting that all are abducted, but many of these people may well have been. If this is the case, I would guess that most have probably been turned into the alien food I described earlier.

What about the people who survive and are returned safely to Earth? There are millions of people who claim to have been abducted by aliens. Like UFO sightings, many are probably not genuine. However, many very convincing cases have occurred over the years, and these cases have so many things in common, it leads one to believe that these traits are more than just coincidental.

A typical description of abduction starts in one's car, in bed or outdoors with the appearance of a bright light followed by the feeling of complete paralysis apart from being able to move one's eyes. Abductees then describe being "taken up" and placed in a bright circular room where they are involuntarily examined. The examiners are invariably small and grey with very large eyes, often supervised by larger beings. Instruments unlike standard Earth based surgical instruments are used to examine various orifices and take samples of blood, semen or eggs. The victim is totally paralysed throughout, but experiences a telepathic connection with the alien beings. Often victims remember the controlling influence of the large dark coloured alien eyes, and sometimes describe tiny implants being inserted into the nose, arm, head, neck or foot. These implants are possibly some kind of tracking device. After the experience victims cannot account for the time during which the abduction took place, often described as missing time. It is believed that the aliens induce a mental block in the victim's brain so that all memories of the event are obscured. Victims usually recall the events under hypnosis or in dreams, which is often many months after the event.

Many victims have undergone hypnosis as a means to get to the truth behind their experiences. There is some controversy however over whether hypnosis reveals the truth or whether it simply encourages more fanciful made up scenarios in the persons mind. There is huge debate about whether the abduction phenomenon is real or not, I could go into individual cases to support the claim one way or another. The problem with abductees is that they all seem to have memory loss of the abduction event itself so it's very easy for sceptics to dismiss their accounts as dreams or even just attention seeking. Rather than unravel individual abductee's accounts, I would like to mention a person whose evidence relating to alien abductions cannot be dismissed as a dream or otherwise.

Over the last 12 years or so, American surgeon Dr Roger Leir has removed several suspected alien implants from patients. All of the patients claim to have had abduction experiences. On 23rd September 2006 he removed his 12th implant from the toe of a 45 year old woman.

Leir explains the common characteristics of implant removals he has undertaken in recent years. No evidence of how the implants got inside the body are present, that is, there is no scarring. When the soft tissue around the object is examined there is no inflammatory response which, according to Dr. Leir, is impossible, because any foreign body which is implanted into the body should result in an inflammatory response. Implants are surrounded by a large number of nerve receptors which are not anatomically correct. One implant which he removed consisted of a grey biological membrane; a tiny sack about 7mm in diameter, which when cut open contained a further grey membrane. This inner membrane was so tough it could not be cut open by a surgical scalpel. Inside this inner membrane was a tiny triangular object.

The object was sent for metallurgic testing at Los Alamos laboratories, who tested the item and then recommended further testing. The object was then analysed by New Mexico Tech laboratory, who had not been told that the object was removed from a human body. The laboratory reported that the object contained elements so rare, that the object was probably a fragment of a very rare meteorite, only a few of which have ever been discovered on Earth.

Further examination under an electron microscope, found that the implant did not have a natural structure and was in fact a manufactured item, therefore was not part of a naturally occurring meteorite at all. The examination also revealed that the object had been connected to the patient's nerve endings. The laboratory later concluded that elements found in the sample were extraterrestrial and did not occur naturally on Earth.

Further research by Dr Leir has revealed that the implants give off radio waves. Using a guass meter [a device for measuring radio waves] he measured radio waves at two different frequencies coming from the implant whilst still inside the patient's body. As for figuring out how the implant works, our scientists have no explanation. It seems that the device actually interfaces in some way with nerve endings.

What I find very strange about Dr. Leir's findings is that the U.S. Government and media do not appear to be interested. Governments should be very concerned about these claims and should spend public money in order to get to the bottom of the mystery. I suspect that the U.S. Government knows about the phenomenon and knows there is nothing they can do about it. This is possibly why they turn a blind eye to the subject.

So what might these implants be for? I would suggest they are either for monitoring or controlling the person or aspects of the person that is fitted with the device. The next question is why? Why monitor or control a selected number of human beings on our planet?

I do not have an answer to this question, but if we consider what we have learned about alien beings so far I doubt that their motives are particularly beneficial to the human race. Perhaps when they abduct a person, they collect a sample of their DNA [the blue print or building block of life, **03**], and then catalogue the subject. Perhaps they then monitor how that person develops in the future. Do they have resistance to certain viruses? Do they have the particular characteristics the aliens are looking for in their genetics programme? Maybe very few subjects comply with their specific needs, which is why they need to monitor so many in order to find the ones they require. I can't help thinking that it is in some way to do with their programme to correct their own genetic problems I mentioned earlier.

Another possibility is that one day, all of the people in our population that are fitted with implants will suddenly turn into foot soldiers working for the aliens to take over the Earth. The real reason for these implants may become clear in the future, but for now all we know is that there are many people walking about the Earth who have alien implants in their bodies. The vast majority of abductees, that have been returned to the Earth, probably do not know they have been abducted and have therefore never mentioned it to anyone. Some of Dr. Leir's patients only discovered they had an implant after a routine X-Ray. Now consider that 4 million

Americans claim to have been abducted by aliens, how many millions might be fitted with an alien implant?

The fact that aliens can abduct human beings, then perform surgical procedures on them without any resistance is quite worrying. It means they can exercise a degree of control over our mind that renders us totally helpless. But hang on a minute, are we not being a little hypocritical by taking offence at being "tracked" by aliens. Consider, if you will, our scientists that study animal behaviour, who often attach radio tracking devices to record the movements and mating habits of different Earth species. They fire a dart containing anaesthetic to immobilise some unsuspecting creature, then fit the device before releasing the animal back into the wild. An hour or so later the lion wakes up and trots off having no recollection of the event, newly fitted with an appendage it does not understand. Does this not sound familiar?

Many abductees claim to undergo repeat abductions throughout their lives. These people are often first abducted in childhood and possibly fitted with an implant, which might be to allow the aliens to find the abductee at some point in the future. However, Dr. Leir does not believe the devices are used to find the individual in the future, he believes the aliens can do this without an implant. The reasons why aliens would need to abduct the same person more than once is not understood. One possible reason is that the programme they have for correcting their own genetic defects, involves using the same human over a period of many years. Perhaps they need many humans over a long period in order to mimic the process of evolution in their own laboratories to develop improved versions of hybrid beings.

Whatever mechanism is used to paralyse humans during abduction, the most plausible explanation is that they somehow control our brain. Perhaps some kind of helmet would be able to screen our brain from this controlling influence and thus prevent abduction. To prepare for the future one thing we can consider is something that will protect us against the abduction threat. Somebody that has already considered this problem and invented a device to prevent his brain from being controlled is Michael Menkin. His device, the "Thought Screen Helmet", prevents telepathic communication between humans and aliens and can be constructed in just 4 hours. Menkin claims that aliens cannot immobilise people wearing thought screens nor can they control their minds or communicate with them using their telepathy. In an emergency, when you do not have your "Thought Screen Helmet" to hand, I would recommend using a metal biscuit tin instead.

# 6. Where do they come from and why?

So, where do these aliens come from, and why? How many of them are there? How many planets do we known are inhabited by aliens? Do they play backgammon?

When I say that the aliens come from a particular star, this is not strictly true. Our own sun is in fact a star, and around it the Earth and other planets orbit. We humans live on a planet orbiting a star called the Sun. Aliens that come from other places also live on planets orbiting their own star; their star is essentially the same as our sun, sometimes their star is smaller but often much larger. So when I say the aliens come from a particular star it means they are from a planet which orbits that star.

In the previous chapter on aliens I mentioned names of stars or star systems where the aliens come from. In order to fully understand where these places are I need to explain a little about the place we know as "outerspace" or "the Universe".

Most people do not have any feel for the geography of outerspace because they don't need to know about it in their everyday lives. I mean it's not very often we need to go to Saturn to watch a football match or a moon of Uranus to attend a birthday party. We know the continents of the Earth and the countries within them. Most of us have good knowledge of our planet. So what about other worlds, where are they?

I will start at the Earth and go outwards until I have described the known Universe, that is, everything, then I will come back and explain where aliens are from. You might be surprised. Our Earth orbits the Sun once a year. There are several other planets also orbiting our sun. The Sun and this group of planets are called our "solar system". The size of our solar system is about 7000 million miles across, which sounds a lot but is tiny compared to the distance of the nearest star.

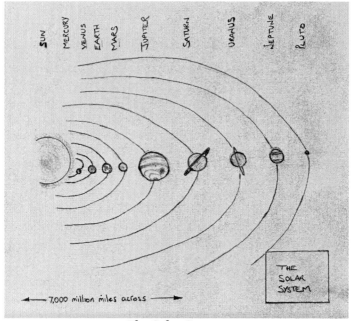

The Solar System

In order to describe how far away the nearest star is, we measure the distance in light years. One light year is the distance you would travel if travelling at the speed of light for one year [the speed of light is described by current physics text books as the fastest possible speed anything can travel, which is 186,000 miles per second]. One light year if represented in miles is 5.7 million million miles [or 5.7 trillion miles].

Although our solar system is 7000 million miles across, this is only a tiny fraction of a light year. The nearest star to Earth is 4.3 light years away [which is about 4,000 times the distance across our solar system]. Stars which are considered to be close to our sun would be in the region of 4 to 500 light years away. Moving outwards further, our sun is one of 200 billion other stars, in what is called our galaxy.

The galaxy is a spiraling, rotating bulging mass of stars all rotating around a common centre. Our galaxy, known as the Milky Way Galaxy, is 100,000 light years from end to end.

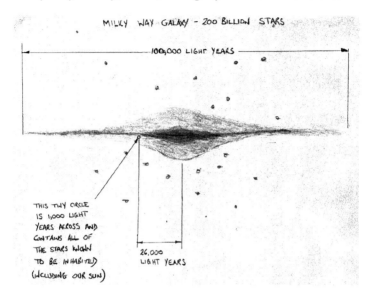

MILKY WAY GALAXY - 200 BILLION STARS

100,000 LIGHT YEARS

THIS TINY CIRCLE IS 1,000 LIGHT YEARS ACROSS AND CONTAINS ALL OF THE STARS KNOWN TO BE INHABITED (INCLUDING OUR SUN)

26,000 LIGHT YEARS

Our Galaxy – The Milky Way

It doesn't end there! There are over 50 billion galaxies like our Milky Way in the Universe. The nearest galaxy to our Milky Way galaxy is the Andromeda galaxy, which is 2.2 million light years away. The furthest galaxies that we know of in the Universe are in the region of 1,000 million light years away, and the Universe is estimated to be around about 1,000 million light years in size. Phew!.

Now that we have a grasp on the sizes, you may wish to read through the last section again, it turns out that all of the alien populated stars I mentioned earlier are inside our own Milky Way Galaxy! Not only that, they are all within 500 light years of our sun. In other words, in galactic terms they live on the same street!

Below is a table showing the distances from the Earth of the stars that the aliens come from.

| Race | Star | Distance (light years) |
| --- | --- | --- |
| Small Gray | Zeta Reticulum | 39 |
| Small Gray (brown) | Bellatrix | 240 |
| Large Gray | Betelgeuse | 427 |
| Indigenous Reptilian | Sun | 0 |
| Draco Reptilian | Alpha Draco | 215 |
| Sirians | Sirius B | 8.6 |
| Anunnaki | Sun (Nibiru) | 0 |
| Nordics | Pleiades | 385 |

You might be asking, how on Earth can they travel these distances bearing in mind it would take 39 years to get to Zeta Reticulum at the speed of light? To answer this I will refer back to Bob Lazars information on alien spaceships. The crafts he describes can exceed the speed of light. In fact they can achieve speeds many times the speed of light by using their gravity based propulsion systems. It is claimed that the journey to Zeta Reticulum takes 91 days, which works out at a speed 160 times the speed of light.

Looking at the table above, there are two races that are zero light years from the Sun. The first are the Indigenous Reptilians whom are believed to originate from Earth, and were described in a previous chapter. The second are the Anunnaki who inhabit a planet in our solar system which is believed by many to be in a highly **elliptica**l [non circular or oval] orbit around our sun. Allegedly, the planet orbits the sun once every 3600 years. There is a great deal of speculation about this planet, and whether it is headed towards us in years to come.

What do we know about these other worlds?

## Zeta Reticulum – Home of the Small Gray

Zeta Reticulum is a binary star. This means there are two suns similar to our own which orbit around each other. The second of these two stars is known as Zeta 2 Reticuli and is believed to have planets orbiting it as our sun does. The Small Grays are believed to inhabit the fourth planet around this star. The planet is believed to be a third larger than Earth, which means it has 75 percent more surface area. One year on this planet is believed to be longer than an earth year, and a day is about 90 hours long. The planet is physically similar to Earth, but colder, with a thinner atmosphere, and a higher proportion of helium and argon. Other than the information given here it is not possible to say what the world is like on the surface. Zeta Reticulum can only be seen from Earth if you live in the southern hemisphere, that is, if you live south of the equator. I have drawn a star map so that you can identify this star in the night sky [see southern star map below].

Up until the mid nineties, mankind had not observed any planets other than the ones in our own solar system. We knew about other stars, but had no way of knowing if planets existed around these far away stars. This is because, up until then, telescopes were not powerful enough to see planets, only stars. A project was started in the 1980's to build a telescope that would be capable of observing these far away planets. This telescope is called The Hubble Telescope and is a space telescope. This means that the telescope is in orbit around the Earth and does its observing outside of the Earths atmosphere. Because the telescope is outside of the Earths atmosphere it can see objects much clearer than it would on the ground. The telescope was launched in 1990, but was plagued by technical problems to do with the large mirror that it used. It was repaired by astronauts in 1993. In 1995 the Hubble Telescope observed a planet orbiting another star. To date there have been around 300 planets observed orbiting other stars. In 1996 it was reported that a planet had been discovered orbiting one of the Zeta

Reticulum stars. This was reported on the Extrasolar Planets Encyclopedia website. The information was withdrawn from the website just 4 days after publication and it was announced that the discovery had been a mistake. By a huge co-incidence, in Bob Lazars video, which was made in 1990, Lazar claims that the Small Gray aliens originate from a planet in the Zeta Reticuli star system! It is as if NASA [National Aeronautics and Space Administration, **21**] released the information as it normally would when it discovers a new planet, then realised by doing this were confirming Bob Lazar's story, and so in panic withdrew the findings.

## Betelgeuse – Home of the Large Gray

The Betelgeuse star is massive, 800 times larger than our sun. There is very little known about the planet itself. One thing that we can surmise is that a year on a Betelgeuse planet would be equivalent to hundreds of years on Earth. In our sky this star can be seen from the Northern hemisphere and is the second brightest in the constellation of Orion [see northern star map below].

## Alpha Draco – Home of the Draco Reptilian

Also known as Thuban, again little is known about this planet. In the sky the Alpha Draco star can be seen from the Northern hemisphere and is next to the **Big Dipper** [a very well known group of 7 stars, sometimes called "The Plough" or "Ursor Major"]. [see northern star map below].

## Sirius B – Home of the Sirian

This is the closest star to our own sun that is believed to be inhabited. The planets around Sirius B are believed to be inhabited by reptilian and aquatic type life forms. [see southern star map below].

## Nibiru – Home of the Anunnaki

The description of this planet is based on research by **Zecharia Sitchin** [an expert on ancient languages, **50**] and information he derived from artifacts from Sumerian culture which is at least 6,000 years old. There is much evidence in these artifacts, which include stone tablets that indicate that Earth has been visited by the aliens. The Annunaki are a race of aliens, which the Sumerians considered to be their gods. The Sumerian land is known today as Iraq. If we imagine a primitive culture on Earth being visited by an alien race, perhaps descending in a spacecraft, they would probably not describe them as aliens. Remember that ancient races had no knowledge of the Universe, planets or stars. If an alien landed, it would have been considered to be a God or God-like. This is how the Sumerians portrayed the Annunaki aliens.

In 1982 NASA officially recognised the possibility of Nibiru, or Planet X as it is sometimes known, with an announcement that an object is really there, far beyond the outermost planets. It is thought that this celestial body may actually be a brown dwarf [a failed star which emits much less light], or that the brown dwarf has a planet in orbit around it, which is Nibiru.

## Pleiades – Home of the Nordics

According to **Billy Meier** [a Swedish farmer who claims to have been in contact with friendly aliens since he was young, **52**] they number only a little more than 500 million on their Terra-formed planet of Erra, in the "Taygeta" system of the Pleiades. This suggests that they have probably been living on that planet for a relatively short period of time compared with the inhabitants of the Earth, who number over 7 billion. They also claim to have horses, cows, rabbits, fish, and other "Terran" life-forms roaming about on their planet. This strongly suggests that the ancestrage of the Pleiadeans and those on Earth are intimately linked via ancient civilisation.

The Pleiades can be seen from the Northern hemisphere in winter and the Southern hemisphere in summer. [see northern star map below].

## How to identify these stars in our sky

It might be useful to be able to recognise the different stars in the sky that aliens come from. It would certainly be one way of breaking the ice with an alien. Pointing to his home in the sky might just warm him to you a little. Or perhaps you could just use it to impress your friends when walking home from the pub. If you wish to view these stars in the night sky I have drawn two star maps. The first map pertains to the northern hemisphere night sky and the second, the southern hemisphere sky.

All of the stars I have mentioned are easily visible with the naked eye. I suggest going to a dark place well away from city lights, preferably on a night with clear skies.

# Northern Star Map

Betelgeuse (Large Gray) , Alpha Draco (Draco Reptilian) , Pleiades (Nordics) (winter only)

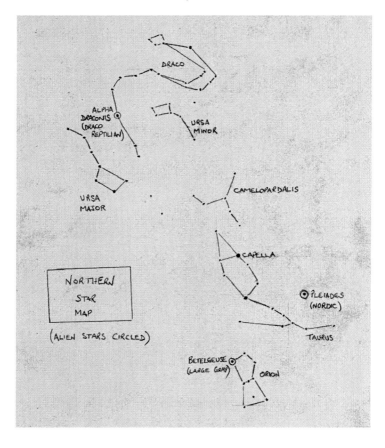

## Southern Star Map

Zeta Reticuli (Small Gray) , Sirius (Sirians)

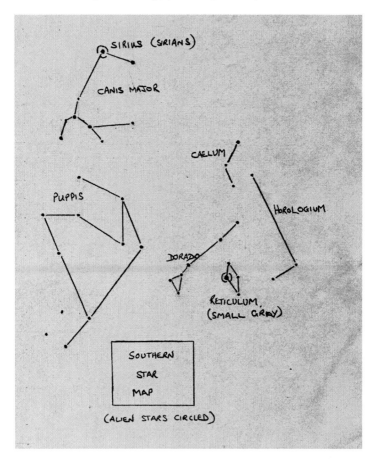

# Why do they come here?

What follows is a selection of probable reasons for the existence of aliens on this planet. The reasons discussed are generally accepted in the UFO community and are derived from a range of sources.

## *To correct problems in their evolution*

The Small Gray alien is an ancient race and because of their particular evolution, or lack of evolution they have encountered problems with their physiology. They have a non functioning digestive system and have developed other ways of ingesting food. Their bodily reproduction systems no longer function and they have developed cloning techniques to produce new life. The continual use of cloning has weakened the species and they are seeking ways to correct this. One activity they are involved with on Earth is a project to use human DNA [the blueprint or building block of life, **03**], which they consider healthy, to produce hybrid species which have less of the problems of the original Gray alien.

It is also rumoured that a deal was made between the American Government and the Large Grays when President Eisenhower disappeared during one of his regular golfing weekends early in 1954. This deal was to include a non-interference of races in exchange for technology, and that obligated the U.S. Government to provide 75 underground bases the construction of which would start some time in 1959. The Grays returned in 1954 in very large numbers in one ship and many smaller shuttles to **Edward's Air force Base** [a US Air Force Base, **23**].

## *To utilise the Magnetics of the Earth*

Other reasons cited about why aliens are on Earth are to do with the magnetic properties of the Earth. It has long been suspected by many scientists that **natural magnets** [the type we all played with at school and were fascinated by the attractive and repulsive properties, **07**] posses a built-in ability to produce energy. Mainstream science hasn't really found a good use for magnets apart from sticking them on fridge doors. However it is believed that the aliens do have a use for this type of magnetism. It is thought, by some scientists, that natural magnets could provide a limitless source of energy if we only knew how to build a machine to tap into that energy. A lot of alien technology is rumoured to be based on magnetism, as opposed to our technology which uses electricity and wires to transfer energy and provide control. Their systems do not need wires to transmit power and provide control and use magnetism instead. Not only may they be here because of natural small magnets, but because the Earth itself is a large magnet. **Thomas Valone** [a leading scientist on energy, **43**] states that magnetics are related to **zero point energy** [the energy believed to be locked within space itself, known as the quantum vacuum, **05**]. What they do with this is anyone's guess. Perhaps they somehow export energy?

## *To prepare our planet for their occupation*

A further reason for alien occupation could be that the worlds they inhabit are dying and their mission here is to prepare the Earth so that they can emigrate to it. Rather like the British in the late 1700's preparing Sydney for a prison population. Rather than just eject us from the planet, they are subverting our power structures, namely the U.S. shadow government and the **U.N.** [United Nations, **22**] so that they can take control without a major disturbance or without us even realising it is happening. According to Phil Schneider part of the alien agenda is to reduce the Earths population by $5/6^{th}$ to $7/8^{th}$ of the current population by 2029. He further states that the alien agenda is to create a single world government which they would then control. And finally, that the remaining humans would be used as slaves in a planet controlled by aliens.

### To create hybrid species for specific purposes

Other theories postulate that aliens have come to Earth to use advanced genetic engineering techniques to create a new hybrid warrior breed for a war at some nearby star.

### To change our evolution so that we can be "used"

I touched on this one earlier. It is rumoured that hundreds of thousands of years ago man was created by tampering with our evolutionary process in order to create a slave race that could do work for a previous race living on the Earth. And the human race is in fact descended from this slave race. This is a reason why we earthlings are considered low on the intelligence scale by alien races. They look down on our intelligence, as we would look down on a chimpanzee's intelligence.

### To be used as containers

A chilling piece of information that Bob Lazar quotes from the briefing documents about the aliens, is that humans are used as "containers". He then goes on to say that he does not know what this means. One answer could be that we are containers of information in the form of DNA. Our scientists are only just beginning to unravel the complexities of our DNA. A large amount of the DNA information in our bodies is redundant. What capabilities or information could be locked away in this genetic code? Could there be something that is being contained by our very own cells that the aliens are interested in?

If we pause for a moment and consider the reasons why aliens are here and ask the question, would aliens want the human race to know about their occupation here on Earth? I think the answer would emphatically be no. If the population thought for one minute that any of the above were happening, who knows what the reaction would be. It is in the alien's interests to remain hidden, at least for now, until they fully subvert the worlds existing power structures.

As for the backgammon question, if they did play they would most certainly beat humans due to their superior intelligence and logical thought pattern.

# 7. Technology

Some technology that we earthlings use on Earth today was produced as a result of the U.S. military and other corporations studying alien technology given to them by aliens or recovered from UFO crashes. Therefore we have already had technological changes on the Earth due to the existence of aliens. I will deal with this first before I move on to the unseen technology that might appear in the future. According to **Philip J. Corso** [an American U.S. Army officer, **48**] extraterrestrial artifacts were recovered from the crash at Roswell in 1947, and he oversaw the **reverse engineering** [reverse engineering is when a finished product is examined, in this case UFO artifacts, in order to try and decipher how they work]. This indirectly led to the development of certain "products" including accelerated particle beam devices, fibre optics, lasers, integrated circuit chips and Kevlar material. Kevlar is now a widely used material in bullet proof vests and fiber optic cable shielding. If this is true, it is very significant, after all, fibre optics and the integrated circuit have revolutionized the IT and telecommunications industries which has changed our lives forever.

Undoubtedly alien races have technology which is far more advanced than our own. By considering the simple fact that they have travelled here, leads us to conclude that they are more advanced. I touched earlier on the UFO propulsion system and some of the weapons that aliens are known to possess. When **disclosure** [revealing of the truth behind aliens and UFOs, **08**] of the alien and UFO cover up occurs, and the governments of the world release information of their choosing, what technology might then be revealed? Even when this happens, I would imagine that governments will be very careful about what technology they decide to reveal. I cannot even say that any technology will be revealed. What I can do is describe some of what is known about the technology rumoured to exist, either in the hands of aliens or in the hands of the shadow government.

I will split the different technologies into four groups, namely, energy, transport, magnetics and biology.

**Energy**

Probably the biggest current "hot topic" issue on our planet is energy. We rely on energy in our everyday lives almost every second of the day, and we pay for energy every second of the day too. The electricity that powers everything we need, the gas that heats our home, the fuel we put in our cars and the aeroplanes we love for our holidays and travel. Think of all of the factories that use electricity to produce the precious goods that we all crave. It is the use of energy which is damaging our planet through global warming.

Of all the energy we use on Earth, the following is a breakdown of the various sources from which the energy is derived:

| | |
|---|---|
| OIL | 37% |
| COAL | 25% |
| GAS | 23% |
| NUCLEAR | 6% |
| BIOMAS | 4% |
| HYDRO | 3% |
| OTHER (Including solar, wind etc) | 2% |

Looking at these figures, if we take the first 4, they being, oil, coal, gas & nuclear, they amount to over 90% of the world's energy use. All of these fuels involve digging holes into the ground and then transferring large amounts of "stuff" from the ground to a place that can then convert the "stuff" into energy. The first 3, they being, oil, coal and gas represent 85% of the worlds energy use, and are allegedly killing our planet by producing the global warming gas, carbon dioxide.

In the United States today, energy use represents 11% of **GDP** [Gross Domestic Product, **09**]. In other words, out of all the money spent 11% goes on digging stuff out of the ground and converting it to the energy we need. Some claim this figure is much higher, nearer 20%.

11% of U.S. GDP is a massive amount of money, and some people have become very rich and powerful because they have profited from a world which relies totally on digging these resources out of the ground. What must be borne in mind when considering whether we could replace the current energy delivery systems of our planet into something completely new or different are two things: the first is that the rich, powerful people that control our energy delivery are to a large degree either indirectly or directly in control of our governments. Secondly, if we did replace the world's energy systems with something different, the period of transition from one method to another could be quite traumatic in the short term. I shall illustrate these problems with a simple analogy.

There is a large mountain ahead of us in our journey of progress, and if we climb over the mountain, on the other side there is a much better place to live. However, there are people on this side of the mountain blocking the way, because it is not in their interest for us to go there and they are stopping us by using every way they can from going any further up the mountain. The people blocking us are the oil cartels; the mountain is the changes we need to endure to re-design our energy systems, and the pastures over the hill are "free energy".

What is "free energy"? Free energy is sometimes called **zero point energy** [05], and is believed by many leading scientists, such as Thomas Valone, to be the ability to extract energy from the "quantum vacuum" or space itself, or from nothing! Researcher **Nikola Tesla** (1856 – 1943) [51], widely regarded as Americas greatest electrical engineer was the first to suggest the possibility of free energy. Here is a quote of his from 1891,

"Throughout space there is energy. Is this energy static or kinetic? If static our hopes are in vain. If kinetic then it is a mere question of time that man will succeed in attaching their machinery to the very real work of nature. Many generations may pass but in time our machinery will be driven by a power obtainable at any point in the Universe".

Many believe that this technology is the energy source that aliens have mastered and that our shadow government knows far more about it than is presently understood by mainstream science.

Another technology that interested Nikola Tesla was the **wireless transmission of energy** [this is the ability to send power or energy from one place to another, as we do currently with electrical cables or power lines without using cables or power lines. i.e., sending the energy through space as we do with radio signals]. The FBI confiscated all of Tesla's research notes when he died, claiming there were 3 possible military applications for his work. According to **Al Bielek** [who was involved with secret government projects, **53**], the military have developed a magnetic weapon device derived from the Tesla research which uses 2 crossed magnetic beams and has been used to shoot down UFOs. According to Bielek they have tested the device by firing it from Earth at the moons of Jupiter.

Thinking back to the chapter on UFOs and the way they stay off the ground, the craft do require lots of energy. It could be that some of the craft use zero point energy to provide this necessary power. The craft which Bob Lazar worked on did not use zero point energy and instead used an antimatter reactor to produce the necessary energy. The antimatter reactor is described later.

If this kind of energy was made widely available and the world was converted to run on it, there would be no need for oil, coal, gas or any of the other types of energy. Not only that, a zero point energy device might not give off any pollutant material and therefore solve the Earth's global warming problem. The main problem with this kind of energy for the "powers that be" is that it is difficult to meter or measure how much people are using and therefore impossible to make money from it. Once a person has the capability to build this kind of machine, they can then power their house, car or anything from it themselves and stop relying on a third party to supply them. This means the third party cannot make money from them. Consider your current energy use, it is all metered. The gas and electric meters in your house and the meter which measures the fuel going into your car at the petrol pump. This is one reason why the technology has not been released. In theory it would be possible to have a device installed in your house that could produce limitless quantities of energy forever. This is a dream come true for the consumer, but for the money making energy giants it is the end of the world. No metering, no revenue, therefore no power. Another possible reason why this type of technology is suppressed by our governments is for purely military reasons. By giving the public the ability to harness massive quantities of energy out of nothing, might mean that some people would use the same technology to make weapons. These weapons might be far superior to the conventional weapons we have today.

If the technology was made available, how would the technology be introduced? My prediction is that we would initially use a lot of the infrastructure that is already available. For example, if we consider a house which currently uses a **240 volts electricity supply** [the type of electricity used by most households]. A device that I will call a "domestic conversion kit" could be sold. We would then disconnect the house from the incoming electricity supply and connect it to the "domestic conversion kit". The device would then provide the required 240 volts electricity supply "forever", resulting in limitless energy and no bills. This way all of your household appliances would not need to be replaced and would operate as normal. Any devices which use a battery, such as a mobile phone, flashlight or power tools could be fitted with a battery that lasts forever.

The technology could be used to design a new generation of clean engines for cars, planes, and trains etc., that never require fuel! On the other hand, it may well be that we no longer need cars, planes and trains, as they might be replaced by anti-gravity powered vehicles which I will describe later.

Something else to consider is the size of a free energy generator that could be realistically produced, not the physical size, but the actual power output. I mentioned that a "domestic conversion kit" may be possible which would probably need a power output of 20 Kilowatts [enough to power a house] for example, or an ever lasting battery which may have an output of 100 watts [enough to power a flashlight]. It may be the case that rather than having these smaller devices, it is easier to build very large free energy generators, lets say one per town or city, which can generate Megawatts [millions of watts, enough to power thousands of houses] . In order to distribute this energy we could use our existing unsightly power lines that stretch the length and breadth of the country. Or we could transmit this energy through the air, which is exactly what Nikola Tesla was experimenting with back in the first part of the twentieth century. Not only may there be the ability to produce clean free energy, but also the technology to transmit it about the country and world without the need for a distribution system of heavy, cumbersome wires and pylons. In the section on magnetics I will explain the alien's interest in and use of magnetisim, which Nikola Tesla was working so hard to achieve.

In summary, technology already exists which if introduced to our world could totally revolutionise the way we extract, harness and distribute energy. Not only that, it could solve the current crisis of global warming.

**Transport**

I will split this next section into 2 parts: travel below ground and travel above ground.

## Travel Below Ground

Phil Schneider, whom I mentioned earlier in the book, was a key figure employed by the U.S. government (or shadow government) in building underground bases in the U.S. and all over the world. According to Schneider these bases are extremely large, like nothing that exists in the civilian world. They are in the order of cubic miles in size. A cubic mile, hollowed out underground, is huge. Imagine a cube stretching a mile below the earth, a mile long and a mile wide. This is a vast amount of space. Schneider claims that some of the underground bases are bigger than a cubic mile, and that some are in fact four and a half cubic miles in volume. He claimed that there are 131 of these bases in, or under, the U.S. alone and 1,477 worldwide. He also stated that the bases are connected by a network of high speed underground rail links, miles beneath the Earth. The trains or shuttles use a **magneto levitron vehicle** [meaning they float in the air a small distance off a rail using magnetic levitation] and are capable of speeds in excess of **Mach 2** [which is 1,522 miles per hour!]. For illustration this means they could travel between New York and London in just 2 hours.

Thomas Castello, who also claims to have witnessed these underground rail systems, when asked where the trains operate to and from replied,

> "Where?, Everywhere!, They criss-cross the world as an endless subterranean highway. Like a freeway, except this one is underground".

Schneider in his lectures also talked about the advanced boring machines that were used to make the tunnels. He states that the technology used in these machines is far beyond any technology used in construction in the civilian world.

So there we have it, an advanced network of underground railway tunnels right beneath our feet. We can only imagine whether or not these secret tunnels will become part of our everyday lives in the future. Personally I doubt it.

### *Travel above ground*

UFOs are known to use anti-gravity systems to get from A to B. If the technology in these craft has been deciphered, and at some point in the future is made available to us, one can barely imagine the changes in our world that would follow. It would mean the capability to travel anywhere on our planet within a matter of seconds.

The best testimony for the operation of these craft comes from Bob Lazar.

> "The craft sits 16 feet tall and 52 feet, 9 inches in diameter. The exterior skin of the disc is metal which is the colour of unpolished stainless steel. The sport model sits on its belly when its not energized and not on the stereotypical tri-pod legs that folklore usually associates with this type of craft. As you can see the entry hatch is located on the upper half of the disc, with just the bottom portion of the door wrapping around the center lip of the disc. The interior of the disc is divided into 3 levels. The lower level is where the 3 gravity amplifiers and their wave guides are located. These are the integral components of the propulsion system that are used to amplify and focus the gravity A wave."

> **"The Reactor** is located directly above the 3 gravity amplifiers on the centre level and is in fact centered between them."

> **"The Centre level** of the disc also houses the control consoles and seats, both of which were too small and too low to the floor to be functional for adult human beings. The walls of the centre level are all divided into

archways. At one point in time, when the disc was energised, one of the archways became transparent and you could see the area outside of it just as if the archway was a window. Then, a form of writing which was unlike any alphabetic, scientific, or mathematical symbols Lazar had ever seen, began to appear on the one side of the transparent archway. Lazar was never given access to the upper level of the disc so we can't illustrate what the porthole like areas are. We can however assure you that they are not portholes."

The website goes on to explain the operation of the reactor itself which powers the craft,

"The power source is a reactor which uses element 115 as its fuel. In this reactor element 115 is used as a target and is bombarded with protons in a small, highly sophisticated particle accelerator. When a proton fuses into the nucleus of an atom of 115, it is transmuted and becomes an atom of element 116. Although we too can transmute elements here on Earth, it is typically not done in this fashion, or at anywhere near this level of efficiency. Furthermore, we have yet to produce anything heavier than element 112."

"As soon as each atom of 115 is transmuted into 116, it immediately decays and produces a radiation unlike that which we normally observe in nuclear decay. Each atom of element 116 decays and releases 2 antiprotons (anti-hydrogen), a form of **antimatter** [the opposite of matter, **o2**]. Antimatter can be produced in particle accelerators here on earth, but only in minute quantities and only stored for short periods of time."

"The flux of antimatter particles produced in the reactor are channelled down an evacuated, tuned tube (which keeps it from contacting with the matter that surrounds it) and reacted with a gaseous matter target. This total annihilation reaction is the most efficient and energetic nuclear reaction there is. The more familiar nuclear reactions are fission, producing energy from the splitting of atoms as used in nuclear reactors & atomic bombs, and fusion, the fusing or combining of atoms (typically hydrogen nuclei) to release even more energy. Fusion is the reaction that powers the Sun and other stars and is what gives hydrogen bombs their "punch". These two more common nuclear reactions are dwarfed by the power and efficiency of the annihilation reaction used in the alien reactor."

"The reaction between the gaseous matter target and the antimatter particles produces a continuous release of tremendous amounts of heat. This heat is converted directly into electricity by the use of a thermionic generator. The thermionic generator used in this reactor is so efficient, that there is no detectable waste heat produced. This is an apparent violation of one of the basic laws of thermodynamics. Similar, but not nearly as efficient or powerful, thermionic generators are used as power sources in our satellites and space probes."

"As amazing and efficient as all this seems, it is only secondary to the primary function of the reactor. The antiparticle flux emitted from the transmuting element 115 is not the only energy radiated during operation. This is the point at which the gravity A wave is first produced. The gravity wave emitted by the 115 reaction appears on the hemisphere of the reactor, propagating up the tuned waveguide in a fashion very similar to the way microwaves behave."

"All of the actions and reactions inside the reactor are orchestrated perfectly like a tiny little ballet, and in

84

this manner, the reactor provides an enormous amount of power used to amplify the gravity A wave so it can cause the requisite space/time distortion required for space travel."

"Since the shortest distance between 2 points is a straight line, so in our Universe we've always assumed that the fastest way from point A to point B was to travel in a straight line between the 2 points at the speed of light. Well, the fact is that when you're dealing with space/time and you enjoy the capability of generating an intense gravitational field, the fastest way from point A to point B is to distort, or warp, or bend the space/time between points A and B, bringing points A and B closer together. The more intense the gravitational field, the greater the distortion of space/time and the shorter the distance between points A and B."

Summarising the above, the craft generates an intense gravitational field which bends the space it wants to travel towards, thus bringing everything much nearer to itself enabling the craft to travel extremely quickly to that point.

The speed of these craft is so fast that we could travel between any points on our Earth possibly within seconds. If this type of travel was made available to everyone, how would our world change? A further point to note here is that the crafts power source comes from the mixing of matter with antimatter resulting in the total annihilation of matter and the release of a massive amount of energy. This is not the same as zero point energy that I postulated earlier.

Little is known about how these craft might be piloted. It is rumoured that the pilot and craft are connected by a headpiece which connects the craft directly to the alien brain. They fly the craft as you would play the piano.

Clark C. McClelland, an aerospace engineer claimed to have been enlightened about the craft by **Wernher von Braun** [a respected scientist who witnessed wreckage from the Roswell UFO crash, **66**]. He claims that Von Braun related how the exterior of the space craft was not metal as we know it, but appeared to be made of something biological, like skin. The description of the craft's interior was bizarre; it was very bare of instrumentation, as if the creatures and the craft were of a single unit.

## Magnetics

I mentioned earlier that some alien technology is known to use "magnetics" as its principal driving force, as opposed to our own Earth based technology which uses electricity and wires.

Here are quotes from Thomas Castello on the technology in use at the Dulce Base,

> "All the elevators are magnetically controlled, even lights in elevators, as well as all lights on all levels are magnetically induced. The light bulbs are not the type bought on the surface, but a totally different type of light system. The illumination found there is a closer match to natural sunlight than any artificial light on the surface world. The shape of the elevators are unique."
>
> "If you have ever seen a Tupperware sugar bowl, you could see the shape copied in the elevator. Sort of like an open ended oval with another half oval on each side. The elevator shaft matches the shape perfectly. The magnetic controls are in the half oval shape. If you could stand in or close to the half ovals, you would feel the slight pull of the power of those magnets. The motion is smooth and silent, there is a nearly unnoticed surge when the motion starts or stops. There are no cables needed, because the lift is magnetic, not electric. Since there are no cables in the elevator cars there is no chance of them falling."
>
> "The aliens use magnetics for everything. They use magnetics as the basic structure for their energy

source. The more you learn about magnetics, the better. The Human Race calls them 'magnets', the aliens call them 'lodestar'. They have been harvesting lodestars [lodestones] for centuries. Not only that, they want all the magnetic power on Earth. They intend to continue harvesting that power, now and in the future. As long as we were only using magnetic power as an oddity, there was no problem. But in recent times, the human race has begun using magnetic power and finding more ways to utilise that commodity. There was a treaty made. In the original treaty, the human race or those who supposedly 'represented' the human race, if you could call it that, didn't mind at all, 'we' considered magnets as hardly more than useless. As people searched for another source for power, we turned to magnetics."

This quote indicates that aliens are very protective over some of their magnetic technology. It seems unlikely therefore that the human race will be allowed to use this technology in the future, or at least without a fight anyway.

**Biology**

One activity I have mentioned in which aliens seem to be more advanced than humans is in genetic engineering. On Earth, we have made many advances in this field ourselves and have managed to make hybrid animals by crossing different species, such as a sheep and goat. When it comes to fiddling with human beings and making a hybrid ape-man for example, we are not so keen. There are rumoured to have been such experiments carried out behind closed doors, and who can be sure what actually goes on?

Because of our moral stance on changing man's genetics for whatever reason, our laws sometimes inhibit the research and activities that can be lawfully carried out. I can assure you that aliens have no such moral or legal barriers. Their research and level of activity in this area is nothing short of rigorous. People who have inside knowledge of the various types of alien, often claim that aliens are hybrid, or indeed part human.

Another interesting development that aliens have allegedly achieved is the way in which they interface with their technology. Consider a human driving a car or operating a machine, a computer perhaps. Usually, the machine is controlled by receiving information into your brain from your eyes, (and ears perhaps), then making decisions with your brain, then using your hands and/or feet to make adjustments to the machine, thus providing control. This is what we call a control loop, involving continuous sensing, decision and action. How could we improve this loop? It can be improved by removing things from the loop, which will make the system act quicker and therefore more responsively. What can be removed from this loop? How about removing our hands, feet, eyes and ears from the loop? Essentially removing our body. In other words attach our brain directly to the machine, think how much more quickly it would operate. This kind of biological technology would require a level of knowledge and expertise more advanced than we currently have. The UFO craft recovered from Roswell [66] is believed to have incorporated this kind of close knit flight control, where the ship is piloted by direct connection to the alien brain.

Further biological technology which is rumoured to have been gleaned from the Roswell UFO and developed for human use, is the technique used to irradiate food in order to keep it fresh for longer.

We can postulate further, in so much as the aliens probably have more knowledge of viruses and diseases. This could be a good or a bad thing depending on how the aliens choose to use their knowledge. Perhaps they have cures for AIDS and Cancer.

## Other Technology

Some further information given by Thomas Castello about technology in use at the Dulce base include security surveillance devices,

> "The basketball size orbs are used for unmanned patrol. They are silent, but when photographing living beings there is a humming sound. The glow that emits light is magnetic aura. This light is in the visible spectrum. You can see the light, but the light does not reflect off anything."

He also gives information about walking through walls.

> "The aliens have mastered atomic matter. They can go through walls like we go through water! It is not magic, just physics. We can learn to do the same thing. It has to do with controlling atoms at will."

## Summary

If we consider the technology that may be released after a UFO disclosure event, assuming we all use it peacefully and sensibly, you can see how the changes could revolutionise our world, the four main pillars being:

Energy    Transport    Magnetics    Biology

Whether these technologies will be revealed to the public is anyone's guess. It seems extremely unlikely that the technology will be just handed on a plate to the human race. A revolution or a war would probably be required to get to that point. The shadow government have seemingly already picked out the few bits of technology they want us to have and kept the best stuff closely under wraps.

# 8. Politics and Religion

On Earth, the majority of us in the West believe that democracy is the best form of government. A political system where everyone has a say, which means the masses can overturn any government that is not up to the job. If we are going to try to predict our future world politics after a disclosure, we need to know whether there has already been some kind of political disclosure between humans and aliens, and if so explain what the interaction has been and where the power lies. I will also attempt to illustrate that the democracy that we hold so dearly has in fact been subverted and our world is anything but democratic. As long as the majority believes they are living under a democratic world, then we are all happy.

Whether we get the technology described in the last chapter will depend on the politics of the Earth. I will cover the religion question later and focus on the politics first. What will the politics of the Earth be like in a world where everyone knows that we co-habit the Earth with the outerspace alien? Will there be a fair, democratic system where we all have equal rights? Or will we be plunged into a kind of repressed new Middle Ages, where we have no freedom and limited wealth?

First of all I would like to mention a little bit of essential history that is not mentioned in any of our history books. Phil Schneider quoted in 1995,

> "Back in 1909 the U.S. cavalry was engaged in catching some bandits that had crossed over the Mexican border into a place called 'Truth or Consequences', New Mexico and they went into a cave or a hideout and killed the so called bandits, but what they found out they couldn't explain. They were called horseshoe craft at that time or horseshoe ships, they were UFOs. They saw these, what they called demons, grey demons, little grey guys around the place, that was in 1909. Now in 1933 our government was actively

engaged with the Europeans mostly the French and the English in special research dealing with aerial phenomenon. Once again the term flying saucer or flying disc didn't come about until much later, supposedly around about the mid 1940's."

In this next quote, Schneider is referring to UFOs which were seen fleeing from the location of nuclear test sites immediately before nuclear bombs were set off.

"Also in 1946 we were engaged in atomic bomb testing in the area of 'Bikini Atoll', some of the pictures here showing the actual language of the U.S. Army and U.S. Navy archives, these flying ships (UFOs) were seen in 1945 and 1946, some of them were called '**foo fighters [10]**', you name it. They were fully known about maybe in 1935 or 1936 by the U.S. Navy."

"This all lead up to later on about 6 to 8 years later, 1954 during the Eisenhower administration lead to an interesting treaty called the Greada 1954 treaty, that was an alien-human treaty. Supposedly the aliens had come in and exchanged technology, and they'd want to take an occasional human being and few cows, accurate books were supposed to be kept, of course eventually all that broke down. Aliens are notorious for being liars, even greater liars than we humans are, alien treaties are not worth the paper they are written on."

When Eisenhower left office in 1961 he made a farewell speech, in it were some interesting passages,

"We face a hostile ideology global in scope, atheistic in character, ruthless in purpose, and insidious in method. Unhappily the danger it poses promises to be of indefinite duration. To meet it successfully, there is called for, not so much the emotional and transitory sacrifices of crisis, but rather those which enable us to carry forward steadily, surely, and without complaint the burdens of a prolonged and complex struggle – with liberty the stake. Only thus shall we remain, despite every provocation, on our charted course toward permanent peace and human betterment."

"In the councils of government, we must guard against the acquisition of unwarranted influence, whether sought or unsought, by the military-industrial complex. The potential for the disastrous rise of misplaced power exists and will persist."

"We must never let the weight of this combination endanger our liberties or democratic processes. We should take nothing for granted. Only an alert and knowledgeable citizenry can compel the proper meshing of the huge industrial and military machinery of defense with our peaceful methods and goals, so that security and liberty may prosper together."

Was Eisenhower trying to warn us about the alien threat?

According to Thomas Castello political involvement between humans and aliens goes back further than 1909. Castello claimed that beneath Mount Shasta in Northern California is an underground city known as Telos City. He claimed that every president in U.S. history has visited Telos City since **Grover Cleveland** [American president from 1885 to 1889 and from 1893 to 1897]. Harry Truman visited the Lower Realms and met "The King of The World" there and gave him the "Keys to the U.S.A.".

Castello states,

"Truman received assurance to new high tech knowledge, and victory over all enemies on Earth. He then was introduced to Samaza and Khoach, aliens from Bootes and Tiphon [Draco], both Reptilian 'kings' or Ambassadors. Truman updated the '100 Treaty', that began in 1933 with President Roosevelt and requested magnetic advance, space knowledge and experiments. Khoach agreed, Samaza partially agreed. He exchanged hostages for genetic experiments and magnetic advance, but vetoed space and beam weaponry."

According to Robert Collins [42], Ronald Reagan met with two aliens on different occasions during his presidency, whom were being held captive by the Government. Reagan made a speech to the United Nations [22] in 1987, which hints at his knowledge of the outerspace alien,

"In our obsession with antagonisms of the moment, we often forget how much unites all the members of humanity. Perhaps we need some outside universal threat to make us recognise this common bound. I occasionally think how quickly our differences, world wide, would vanish if we were facing an alien threat from outside this world."

Reagan is also rumoured to have said to Steven Spielberg after a private showing at the Whitehouse of the film E.T., "There are probably only six people in the room who know how true this is". Reagan also allegedly formed treaties and had dealings with aliens.

So if this is correct there has been some kind of contact between American presidents and aliens since the late 1900's and treaties have been formed without the knowledge of the American people. Presidents Roosevelt, Truman and Eisenhower have all had some form of agreements with residing aliens.

What they did was extremely un-constitutional, and goes against everything that America is about, namely freedom. But, put yourself in their shoes for one moment. Perhaps they did not have much choice. Perhaps they thought they were acting in the interests of America and the world. Perhaps they managed to prevent aliens from taking over the world.

So we know that aliens have made agreements with us in the past but have not kept those agreements. They have been happy to subvert our leaders by making them go against the Earths own systems of democracy and government. They have made our leaders keep secrets and tell lies. This suggests to me that they cannot really be trusted, they are not democratic, and probably do not have a great deal of compassion towards the human race.

In answer to my own question, "will there be a fair democratic system under which we all have equal rights?", aliens allowing humans to have equal rights, would be like humans allowing the chimpanzees to have equal rights. Why would a race which is vastly superior in intelligence give us equal rights? Think of the struggle women and black people had gaining equal rights. It's a hard fact to swallow, but I believe that once a disclosure occurs, democracy as we know it will cease to exist. My belief is that in order to control the human race and ultimately the planet, aliens are quite happy for us to believe that we are in control of our own lives, by letting us think we are in control of our democratic processes. But behind the scenes, the shadow government have been subverted without our knowledge.

Bearing all of this in mind, if a disclosure was announced, I believe that this lie would continue. Our governments would continue to be subverted by the aliens, but this would not be made public. The public at large would be made aware of the alien presence and UFOs, but I do not believe that the true nature of the alien agenda would be revealed. They would only reveal enough information not to cause widespread panic.

Once disclosure occurs, who knows how long it would be before people started to distrust the government and what was being said. This would depend on how well our governments controlled the information. Whichever way you look at it, the whole political situation with aliens is basically a massive pressure cooker. It's just a question of when it will explode.

Here is an interesting quote from Clifford Stone, a U.S. Army Sergeant who has had first hand experience of aliens,

> "I believe what is going to eventually happen is that they will make themselves known and immediately go ahead and try to destroy society as we know society."

> "Well, my suggestion would be to stand up to the Grays. Let them know that this is a free society, that we are not going to sit back and let anyone - be they from outer space or some other foreign country - convert the people of the United States."

When questioned further about the locations aliens use for their political meetings Castello replied,

> "The problem is, most of the meetings are held in military bases or underground. The Groom Lake Facility does fly several alien craft that regularly fly over unpopulated land that go back and forth from several bases, Southern California has several notable areas. Twenty Nine Palms, Lancaster or Chocolate Mountains are well know for such activities"

So, what about religion?, might all of this spell the beginning of the end for religion?

Let us go back in time and look at some of the changes that the Christian religion has had to face. The realisation that the Earth is not flat, the realisation that the Earth is not at the centre of the Universe, the realisation that man evolved from apes and not from Adam and Eve. All of these things could easily be used to argue that Christianity is flawed in terms of the facts that it preaches, or used to preach. However, it is still well and truly alive today. When the outerspace alien arrives, and we all accept their existence, this will probably be just another bump that religion will have to ride over, which I am sure it will.

In a recent radio interview I read out a statement from the Vatican (see page 5 of this book), in which the Vatican stated that the existence of aliens does not contradict faith in God. The presenter then replied, "But surely God created man in his own image", implying that he could not have created aliens and man in his own image, to which I replied that religious people just move the goalposts to suit their own ends.

Whether you take the cynical view that I support, which is that religion will survive by just changing its own rules, or you think that the fundamental essence of religion is true and it merely adapts like anything else as time goes by, religion will survive.

Instead of "God created man", cynics might insist on "God created aliens and apes, the aliens then created man by modifying the apes". You can look at this argument in many other ways. After all religion is essentially just a reflection of mankind itself. It is man's hopes, fears, uncertainties and insecurities all bundled into one. Religion was created from man's own psyche, as a means to help him explain in simple terms the world around him and what everything means. So I guess as long as we are free thinking and seek simple explanations for the world, there will always be religion.

I personally prefer to believe in science.

# 9. Protection

I do not wish to scare anyone, if I have not already done so in previous chapters, but in order to prepare for the future we need to consider some grim scenarios that might face us. Phil Schneider claimed that the U.S. Government (or shadow government) had a programme to build thousands of underground prisoner rail carriages which would operate on the secret world underground transport system described earlier in the technology chapter. He claimed that contracts were awarded to 11 different train manufacturers in the U.S., the total number of train cars to be built was 107,200, each with a capacity to carry 143 people. If we calculate the total number of passengers that could be carried, we arrive at 15 million. He claimed that each seat incorporates shackles for wrists and ankles to hold the prisoner in place whilst on the train. He asserted that at some point in the future, once the alien agenda had been released there may be resistance from large numbers of humans, and the prisoner trains were being built in preparation for this situation. Pause for deep breath and a dram of whisky!

If you then consider the alien Gray diet outlined in chapter 3, it doesn't take a genius to work out what could happen to human prisoners once shackled to their seat. If you were lucky you might be sent for genetic experiments. If you were unlucky your insides would be turned into semolina. If a war against the aliens does break out, do we really think we are going to defeat these advanced beings with pistols and flashlights? In the grand scheme of the Universe, the Earth is less than a grain of sand, and in the grand scale of the Earth, we earthlings are even smaller. It's unlikely that some armed resistance will get us anywhere as mere members of the public.

In any situation like this, where there is uncertainty and threat to your life, one thing that you can do is prepare a secure location, a hideout with food and provisions, and some critical items you might need. I am not saying that you should start ripping up your living room floor boards immediately and start digging a bunker. What I am saying is that if the situation changes in the future, perhaps after a disclosure, and the alien threat becomes a reality, then you might consider building and preparing a sanctuary. It might save your life!

The first thing to decide upon is the location of your dwelling. Try and choose somewhere that is quite remote. If you have land somewhere, an allotment or smallholding perhaps, that would be ideal. If not then you could build it in your garden, or convert your cellar.

I will not go into construction techniques or how to lay bricks here, but I will give a brief description of the requirements. There needs to be enough space for you and your family to live, ideally for many weeks, without a water supply, gas or electricity.

You will need enough water for the family for at least a month. Each person should drink two pints a day - so for this you will need 7 gallons each.

Stock twice as much water as you need for drinking, so that you will have enough for washing. If you do have a water supply, top up your containers every day. However you might want to check, by listening to your radio, whether the water supply is contaminated.

Stock enough food for at least one month. Choose foods which can be eaten cold, which keep fresh, and which are tinned or well wrapped. Keep your stocks in a closed cabinet or cupboard and try to provide some variety. Stock sugar, jams or other sweet foods, cereals, biscuits, meats, vegetables, fruit and fruit juices. Children will need tinned or powdered milk, and babies their normal food as far as possible. Eat perishable items first and use your supplies sparingly.

A radio and plenty of spare batteries might be your only link with the outside world, so take a second spare radio with you if you can. There may or may not be broadcasts made, but it is best to have a radio just in case. Here is a list of items you might overlook, tin opener, bottle opener, cutlery and crockery. Warm clothing, bedding, sleeping bags. Portable stove and fuel, saucepans. Torches with spare bulbs and batteries, candles, matches. Table and chairs. Toilet articles, soap, toilet rolls, bucket and plastic bags. Changes of clothing.

A first aid kit is essential with household medicines and prescribed medicines. The first aid kit should contain at least aspirins or similar tablets, adhesive dressings, cotton wool, bandages, disinfectant, ointment, including 'Vaseline'.

A box of dry sand, cloths or tissues for wiping plates and utensils, a notebook and pencils for messages.

Brushes, shovels and cleaning materials, rubber or plastic gloves, dustpan and brush, toys and magazines.

When it comes to sanitation you will need special sanitation arrangements because there might not be water to waste in lavatories. Containers such as polythene buckets, fitted with covers and if possible improvised seats. It is wise to create a separate sanitation room for obvious reasons.

You will require polythene bag linings for emptying the containers, strong disinfectant and toilet paper. Keep these items outside of the main room in a separate sanitation area.

A dustbin for the temporary storage of sealed bags of waste matter should also be used. Use a second dustbin for food remains, empty tins and other rubbish.

If you have only one dustbin, use that for toilet waste only. Put all other rubbish in plastic bags or paper until you can take it outside.

As you plan the main rooms of your refuge you need also to limit, as far as you can, the dangers from heat and fires. Remove anything which may ignite and burn easily, for example, paper and cardboard. If you have a home fire extinguisher, keep it handy. Keep buckets of water ready in case of fire. Keep any doors closed to help prevent the spread of fire.

In the event of an alien attack, damage to gas, oil and electricity systems could cause serious fire and other hazards. All responsible members of your family should therefore know where and how to turn off gas and electricity supplies at the mains, all gas pilot lights and oil supplies.

If you fear an alien attack, turn off the gas and electricity at the mains; turn off all pilot lights. Turn off oil supplies. Close stoves, damp down fires. Shut windows, draw curtains. Go to your shelter.

You may have casualties from an attack, which you will have to care for, perhaps for some days, without medical help. Be sure you have your first aid requirements in your survival kit. Listen to your radio for information about the services and facilities as they become available and about the type of cases which are to be treated as urgent.

If a death occurs while you are confined to the shelter, place the body in another room and cover it as securely as possible. Attach an identification label.

You may or may not receive radio instructions on what to do, depending if other humans have control of radio broadcasting equipment. If no instructions have been given within 5 days, you should temporarily bury the body as soon as it is safe to go out, and mark the ground.

Listen to your radio at all times. To conserve your stocks of water and food, keep them sealed, covered or wrapped and close the cupboard door.

Water means life. Re-use it for different purposes, using as little as necessary for cooking. Cans of food, pierced through the top, may be heated in a saucepan of water and the same water used several times without cleaning the pan. Used utensils can be cleaned by holding or placing them in the same hot water.

Avoid waste and carry out your sanitation arrangements with care. Keep separate containers for lavatory waste and for other rubbish. Keep all containers covered and keep hands as clean as possible.

One final piece of advice when you build your underground bunker, DON'T TELL ANYONE! This may sound obvious, but it would be quite easy for this to slip out in conversation. If other people know about it and the day arrives when you need it, you will find that the bunker is full of fellow earthlings before you get there. You will also probably need a firearm of some kind, not necessarily to shoot aliens, but to keep other humans out of your bunker.

On an entirely different subject, what about when you crawl out of your shelter after the war is over? Your money may well be worthless. Your bank account will probably no longer exist and your paper money will only be useful for lighting fires or wiping your bottom.

What can be done about this? Probably the best advice here is you must get access to your money in advance, before any troubles or wars begin. Take all of your money out of your accounts, cash in your investments and pensions. Maybe even take out a big loan. With all of this money purchase as much gold as you can, then store it in a hidden secure location.

Gold is probably the only thing which might still have economic value after an event such as an alien war.

# 10. The Future Planet

I have made many claims and statements in this book, many of which have enormous implications for the future. Although you may have learned a lot of new information, it is probably only a fraction of the whole alien existence reality. The alien and UFO mystery is like a big jigsaw puzzle. We currently have about 15% of the pieces in place and can see there is definitely something going on in the picture. The remaining 85% of the pieces have been stolen by my older brother who will not let me see them. Some day we may see the finished picture and know the real truth. Until then we must go on the information we have and try and work it out as best we can.

There is a lot of speculation presently about the year 2012, in particular the winter solstice on 21st December. Many people think this date marks the end of the world and cataclysmic events will occur which will destroy mankind. Some people also thought the world would end in 1999, but it did not. However in 2012 galactic alignment will occur, which should not be overlooked and I will explain why.

The first thing to point out is there are actually two totally different types of alignment which are going to occur, they sometimes get mixed up or misinterpreted.

The first alignment is the passage of our solar system, i.e. the sun and all the planets through the galactic equator. This alignment occurs every thirty three million years and does not occur on an exact date such as 21st December 2012, and in fact takes thousands of years to pass through. However it is thought that we are approaching this central point in the years to come. Our sun and all the planets are in orbit around our galaxies centre, and they take about 230 million years to go round once, this is known as a cosmic year. The galaxy is shaped like a flat disc and is most dense in the central plane. We can divide the galaxy into two halves, the top and the bottom with an imaginary line called the galactic equator. When our sun orbits around the galaxy it actually oscillates slowly above and below the galactic equator, and every 33 million years the solar system passes through this equator. Passing through the densest part of the galaxy is said to increase disturbances on the Earth such as causing more comets, meteors, volcanoes, earthquakes and can cause ice ages. It is interesting to note that the dinosaurs became extinct about 65 million years ago, which is two times the period at which we pass through this point. Having said all of this, there is no exact known date for the passage through the central point, it is very gradual and will probably have no noticeable effects on the Earth, at least in our lifetime.

The second alignment is that of our earths axis with the sun and the galactic centre (the centre of our galaxy), which occurs every 26,000 years and will occur on 21st December 2012. Our Earths rotational axis is not horizontal to the plane of its motion around the sun, it is oriented at an angle of 23 degrees. This causes our seasons and is why summer days are longer than winter days. Not only that, there is in fact a slow circular wobble of the Earth which takes 26,000 years for a complete wobble. When the sun rises on midsummer's day each year, the stars in the sky are shifted a tiny amount relative to the sun, this is due to the wobble. In other words the point at which the Earths axis is aligned to the sun moves clockwise around the sun a tiny amount each year, in fact by one degree every seventy four years. This means that if we look in the sky now at the position of the sun and the stars, then look again in seventy four years, the position of the stars relative to the sun will have changed by one degree. This is known as the precession of the equinoxes, and over a period of 26,000 years the stars rotate 360 degrees relative to the sun thus binging them back to their starting position. The beginning or end of this cycle is considered to be when the Earths axis aligns in a straight line toward the sun and the central point of our galaxy. Many scientists think that this alignment could cause significant effects on the Earth, such as a magnetic pole shift. This is when the Earths magnetic North Pole shifts to the South Pole and vice versa, a bit like if you hold two magnets together and one flips around in alignment with the other.

Over recent years the Earths magnetic field has weakened and many believe this is predictive of a future pole reversal. Magnetic pole shifts have occurred in the past which is confirmed in geological records. What is unclear is how precisely the transition occurs, and what effect this will have on life forms here on Earth. For example, if the Earths field drops to zero during the reversal, dire predictions follow. Many electronic devices could be affected, including damage to near earth orbiting satellites. The effects on life could include birds losing their sense of direction during migration and immune system decline of all species.

The Earths magnetic field provides a protective shield known as the magnetosphere, losing this during a pole shift could cause the atmosphere to become thin, leading to altitude sickness near sea level. Much worse, this magnetic field protects the Earth from deadly cosmic rays which would kill most if not all species on Earth should it disappear. Only those living underground would survive, and we have learned a little about those in this book. Perhaps your underground bunker described earlier could double up as a magnetic pole shift protection zone. Scientists believe the last magnetic pole shift was some 780,000 years ago, which is eerily exactly thirty times the 26,000 year cycle of the precession of the equinoxes.

One final thing to consider before moving off the 2012 debate are the ancient Mayan people whose civilization flourished in what is now Mexico from around 300 to 900 A.D. These people knew about the precession of the equinoxes, and catered for it in their calendar. The calendar consists of cycles within cycles. In the calendar they have "great cycles" known as "baktuns", which are 144,000 days long (394 years). There are thirteen baktuns in total (spanning 5,125 years), and they started their calendar of thirteen baktuns, thousands of years before their civilization began. Also bear in mind, there are only thirteen baktuns, after 13 there is no 14th, and then it supposedly starts again. The last day of the thirteenth baktun, you guessed it, is on December 21st 2012. Not only that, thirteen baktuns is equal to one fifth of the 26,000 year precession period described earlier. There are many questions raised in my mind here.

Why did they start their calendar thousands of years in the past? How could an ancient race with no telescopes determine the exact galactic alignment date of 21$^{st}$ December 2012? Why does the calendar end on the galactic alignment date of 21$^{st}$ December 2012? How did they know that the central point of our galaxy had any significance with respect to its gravitational effects on our solar system?

Many people believe that the Mayans did not devise their calendar themselves, that it had been handed down from previous civilizations, who in turn had it given to them by an alien race.

Considering all of this information it is easy to see why there is so much hoo har about this particular day. It may turn out that nothing significant happens and life on Earth continues as normal. However it is certainly worth bearing in mind when considering a future planet with or without aliens.

I would imagine that the alien beings described in this book have knowledge of the 2012 alignment and the effects it will bring to the Earth, especially if we consider their alleged knowledge and use of Magnetics discussed earlier. Perhaps they are waiting for this to occur and will step in when it happens. Either step in and save us, or step in and take over, or both?

We often hear the expression "paradigm shift" when talking about changes to mankind on our planet. If we go back to a time when man lived in caves, his daily activities would be different to those of today. In those days man relied on hunting wild animals for food and was essentially nomadic, travelling wherever he could to find food. The reason why his behaviour is completely different to the man who goes to the office on a Monday morning and switches on his computer, is because of the "paradigm shifts" which have occurred. It is useful to understand these first before considering the future.

The first paradigm shift might be considered to be when man was actually created. I mentioned in an earlier chapter that the Anunnaki alien is rumoured to have created man by genetically modifying an ancient version of man 300,000 years ago. There are many mysteries which seem to support this theory. One mystery is that there are no direct anthropological links between homo sapiens (humans) and the primates we are supposed to descend from. Anthropologists that do not support the "alien creation" theory believe there will be a skull which turns up one day that will prove the link between modern man and an ancient primate or homonid, but no such skull has yet been discovered. The homo sapien race sprang into existence quite suddenly without a definite ancestral trace. The second mystery is that homo sapiens only have forty six chromosomes and all other known primates have forty eight. These facts support the view that our race was in part "designed" by aliens who visited Earth. It is a view which is supported in Lloyd Pyes book "Everything You Know Is Wrong". At some point the alien beings left the Earth, and man remained to evolve on his own. I would consider the first paradigm shift to be the creation of man.

After the aliens left, man lived in caves and was a fairly primitive being for many thousands of years. The second paradigm shift to affect mankind occurred about 12,000 years ago. This is when man realised or discovered how to cultivate the land and grow food, which forced him to settle in one place. This meant that man was able to develop much more complex communities. Now that man was not trekking around from place to place in search of wild animals, he was able to develop a more sophisticated way of living. Time could be spent on activities other than hunting. The discovery of agriculture changed man forever. It may not seem like much of a shift to us now sitting in our air conditioned buildings, but at the time it represented a huge increase in the quality of life for human beings. It brought about advances in language, in clothing, in shelter and housing, in rearing animals and in new types of food.

The third paradigm shift of mankind started in the late eighteenth century with the onset of the Industrial Revolution. This marked a major turning point in human society; almost every aspect of daily life was eventually influenced in some way. Instead of labouring in fields with bare hands, man now worked in factories operating machinery, which paved the way for the world in which we live today. Further advances in the twentieth century, in areas such as information technology, result in the lifestyles we all now enjoy.

Although there have been many changes between these 3 paradigm shifts. The discovery of mathematics, and the changes brought to us by advancing civilizations such as the Romans, these 3 shifts I would consider to be the most significant.

Compare life in the year 1750 with life in 2000. The two are mind bogglingly different, this is what we mean by a paradigm shift. A change so large, that it impacts on every single aspect of our lives.

Now get ready for paradigm shift number 4!

Having discussed many of the technological and political changes that could arise, how can we paint a picture of life in the future? Knowing what we know about ourselves, about aliens and about hidden technology, what might a future world be like?

As I stated at the very beginning of this book I am not going try and predict the future. Remember how all those before us have tried and got it wrong!

Why have we been so poor at predicting the future? One answer might be that our minds are so fixed on the present, that we find it hard to shake off our accepted view of the world and predict what the world will be like. Or that the dynamics of change itself are so complex, involving the changing behaviour of millions of people, that no-one is really qualified to make the prediction. In order to search for scenarios of the future, based on the facts revealed in this book, I decided to turn to others. I selected people from various age groups, gave them some of the information revealed in this book and asked them to predict what things will be like in the future.

## Views of the Future

### Mrs Thompson, 63, Whickham, England

"Yes I do think they are more intelligent, my husband has the same views as me. At the moment I can't believe they are living in underground places, and I believe at this moment in time they are trying to contact us. I would hope that they would want to communicate with us in a friendly way and if they are more advanced than us teach us better ways to live and make the world a better place to live in."

"At the moment I would fear them because I don't know anything about them. Why are these sightings happening, there is something out there with more intelligence and they've been here much longer than we have been on Earth. Why now?, why should we be afraid, I wish something would happen, then we will know. The government are definitely hiding it, America especially, and the public should know, the world should know, if things have happened or if aliens have been found or sighted. We shouldn't be ignorant of things like that."

### Pub Landlord, The Chelmsford, Ebchester, England

"From a landlords point of view it would be fascinating, and I would not treat them any different, I would serve them a beer. My cousin is married to a lady from Uzbekistan and her parents have just come over to this country for the first time, they live in a dry, arid country, rocks, desert and my cousin lives in the middle of the New Forest (Hampshire), and the experiences they are having now is like an alien. Streams, lush vegetation, fish and chips."

"Would I like to encounter an alien? yes I bloody would."

### Brian & Margaret Mitchell, retired, Cramlington,

"The world will be a better place when aliens are here, because at the moment everybody's fighting each other, everybody wants a bit of this and a bit of that. If they shared intelligence, as long as it was for good, then we would benefit. I think you would get a lot of reaction from people on Earth."

### Mrs Falkener, 84, Gosforth, England

When asked about whether she would like high speed anti-gravity travel, replied,

"I like to travel slowly and enjoy the scenery."

Does it worry you that aliens may be here?

"Well now you mention it, if it's true, YES, and if they are more intelligent than us, they can rule the world can't they. My mother in law years and years ago said the Chinese are going to rule us."

### Lora and Katie, both aged 12, Castleside, England

"The future depends whether they're evil or not, because they might make you do bad things. It also depends on how many aliens there are, because they might come to our world and eat all the food. If aliens lived here, I think you would have to make a separate part of the world for them, and a separate part for us. As long as China keeps going we will be alright because that's where all our technology is made."

### Ellis Hall, 43, Police Officer, County Durham

"The future is worrying because if at any time aliens can control us, it means we are no longer in control of our own destiny. If it is true, that they can control us, why aren't they doing it now?, which makes me think it's not as worrying. Surely they would control us now before we become more intelligent. Also if they want power, it could lead to worse wars than what there are now."

"If they're here now and they can have an influence, why aren't they stopping the wars that we've already got? If they are with us and helping the 'powers that be' in our world, why can't we find people like Osama Bin Laden? If they can do the things that are claimed, then things like that should be easy to solve."

### Ellis Hall, 17, golfer, County Durham

"The future with aliens will be like when the white people took over the black people and we had slaves. This is because white people had better technology, so we would all be slaves for a while. Eventually they would see the light and say it's wrong, then we'd all live in peace and harmony, however this could take ages."

### Frank Crawford, 45, Electrician, Castleside

"If they're so clever that they can get here from other worlds, they must be much more advanced and therefore could wipe us out and start from scratch if they wished. Why would they need us for anything more than slaves?"

"If they gave technology to us, the first thing we normally do with technology is make weapons, so I'd possibly be more worried for them than us."

"Surely if they breed with us then they wouldn't be themselves anymore, that's not what they would want."

### Lisa Sunley, 39, Civil Servant, Consett

"The future depends what they want from us. If they wanted to mate with humans and reproduce that would be unacceptable. However, if they just want a few pints of blood and DNA for their labs that's different."

### George Dawson, 10, Castleside, England

"There will be a lot more wars and we will be taken as slaves. There will be no sunlight and no electric power to power our electric machines. There will be no roads. Most humans will live to about 50, but if you are helping the aliens you will live to be 900. Aliens have spaceships made out of rocks and skin."

### Rebecca Crawford, 15, Castleside, England

"In the future I believe aliens will be more open than us in getting to know us, because if we don't know or understand something properly our reaction is to just get rid of it. Whereas they've had time to think about it, and they know we're here."

## Finally

In 1969 after the Apollo eleven astronauts returned to Earth after allegedly landing on the moon for the first time, they held a press conference. Neil Armstrong, Buzz Aldrin and Michael Collins sat on a stage in front of an intrigued audience and the world. During this conference it was remarkable to watch how uncomfortable and awkward they appeared. It certainly looked as though they were hiding something. Buzz Aldrin stated in the years to come that Apollo 11 was followed to the moon by a UFO. Rumours also state that they were chased off the moon by UFOs parked on its dark side. This could explain their very awkward demeanour on that day. All three astronauts resigned from NASA soon after their return.

In 1994 on 25th Anniversary of the moon landing, Neil Armstrong made a rare public appearance and gave a short speech to some students,

"Today we have witnessed a group of students among America's best. To you we say we have only completed the beginning. We leave you much that is undone. There are great ideas undiscovered, breakthroughs available to those who can remove one of truths protective layers."

In other words, those that find out the truth behind the cover up of the alien agenda will make great discoveries and breakthroughs. Let us hope that what is undone, turns out to be of benefit to mankind and not be the end of the Human Race as we know it.

THE END

# 11. Index of Terminology, Organisations, People and Incidents

## Terminology

### 01 UFO

Unidentified Flying Object. This is the term given to objects which are observed in the sky, the origin of which cannot be explained. There have been thousands of UFO sightings in hundreds of countries throughout the world. The term does not necessarily refer to an alien craft or space ship, but this is what is usually implied by the term.

### 02 Antimatter

In atomic physics, particles of which matter is made up have a "charge". This charge is either negative or positive. Antimatter is similar to normal matter except the "charge" on particles is the opposite of that in normal matter. Mixing of matter and antimatter leads to the annihilation of both types of matter and the release of a huge amount of energy. Antimatter does not generally exist in our world as it would be immediately annihilated by matter. Mankind has not found a way to generate and control antimatter so that it can be harnessed and used to create energy.

### 03 DNA

Deoxyribonucleic acid is a nucleic acid that contains the genetic instructions used in the development and functioning of all known living organisms and some viruses. The main role of DNA molecules is the long-term storage of information. DNA is often compared to a set of blueprints or a recipe, since it contains the instructions needed to construct other components of cells, such as proteins and RNA molecules. The DNA segments that carry this genetic information are called genes, but other DNA sequences have structural purposes, or are involved in regulating the use of this genetic information.

## 04 Element 115 (or Ununpentium)

All matter in our universe is made up of "elements". There are 117 elements known to man which are listed by chemists in what is known as the Periodic Table. Each element has a different atomic mass determined by the number of protons in the centre of the atom. Element 115 is a heavy element which has 115 protons in its atomic nucleus. This element does not occur naturally on Earth and can only be sourced from other parts of our galaxy. Element 115 is the fuel used in the anti-gravity propulsion system of a UFO craft which Bob Lazar claims to have worked on. The fuel, when bombarded by protons produces a gravity wave which the craft uses for its propulsion. The reason why the Element does not occur on Earth is because the conditions of temperature and pressure which create elements are different within different stars. Our part of the galaxy has not had conditions required to produce this element.

## 05 Zero Point Energy

In physics, the **zero-point energy** is the lowest possible energy that a quantum mechanical physical system may possess and is the energy of the ground state of the system, what does that mean?

It means that if we examine "nothing", i.e. get some "space" and remove all of the contents including the air, thus creating a vacuum, and if we then cool it to absolute zero, (this is the temperature at which all matter comes to a complete standstill) scientists believe that there is still "energy" in this space! It is an energy locked within space itself. Many scientists, such as Tom Valone, believe we could use this power to replace the energy we currently use. It is also sometimes referred to as "free energy".

118

## 06 Universal Law

This is a law believed to be held by some races of aliens. It states that different races of beings throughout the Universe should not interfere in any way positively or negatively with other races.

## 07 Natural magnets

It is possible to create a magnet by passing an electric current through a coil of wire, this is known as an electromagnet. A natural or "permanent" magnet is a material or object that produces a "magnetic field" and stays magnetised without an electric current. Such a magnet is used to hold notes on a refrigerator door. Permanent magnets occur naturally in some rocks, particularly lodestone, but are now more commonly manufactured. A "soft" or "impermanent" magnet is one that loses its memory of previous magnetizations. "Soft" magnetic materials are often used in electromagnets to enhance (often hundreds or thousands of times) the magnetic field of a wire that carries an electric current and is wrapped around the magnet; the field of the "soft" magnet increases with the current.

## 08 Disclosure

It is generally accepted in the UFO community that the existence of aliens and UFOs on Earth is "covered up" by the American "shadow government". There is a great deal written and spoken about the "Disclosure" of the UFO subject and when and whether it will happen. Disclosure would be revealing, to the public at large, information about aliens and UFOs that is not currently admitted by the Government. In UFO circles this is generally just given the term Disclosure.

## 09 GDP – Gross Domestic Product

The **gross domestic product (GDP)** or **gross domestic income (GDI)** is one of the measures of national income and output for a given country's economy. GDP is defined as the total market value of all final goods and services produced within the country in a given period of time (usually a calendar year). It is also considered the sum of value added at every stage of production (the intermediate stages) of all final goods and services produced within a country in a given period of time, and it is given a monetary value.

## 10 Foo-fighters.

This is an early term given to UFOs before the word flying saucer or UFO was used.

# Organisations

## 20 MJ12

**MJ12,** also known as Majic 12, Majestic Trust, M12, MJ 12, MJ XII or Majority 12, is the code name of a secret committee of scientists, military leaders, and government officials, formed in 1947 by an executive order of U.S. President Harry S. Truman. The purpose of the committee was to investigate UFO activity in the aftermath of the Roswell incident - the crash of an alien spaceship near Roswell, New Mexico, in July 1947.

The primary evidence for the existence of a group named Majestic 12 is a collection of documents that first emerged in 1984. The original MJ-12 documents state that the Majestic 12 group was established by order of President Truman on 24 September 1947, upon the recommendation of Dr. Vannevar Bush and Secretary of Defense James Forrestal.

Since the first MJ-12 documents, thousands of pages of other supposed leaked government documents mentioning MJ-12 and a government cover-up of UFO reality have also appeared, sometimes collectively referred to as the "Majestic Documents."

The primary new MJ-12 document is a lengthy, linotype-set manual dating from 1954, called the MJ-12 "Special Operations Manual (SOM)". It deals primarily with the handling of crash debris and alien bodies.

The MJ-12 documents are alleged to date from between 1942 to 1997 and include such matters as the conduct to be used when meeting an alien, diagrams and records of tests on UFOs, memos on assorted cover-ups, and descriptions of the President's statements about UFO-related issues. The documents contain signatures of important people such as Albert Einstein and Ronald Reagan. No more documents have been leaked or released since 1997.

Prior to the MJ-12 documents being leaked, Canadian documents dating from 1950 and 1951 were uncovered in 1978. These documents mention the existence of a similar, highly classified UFO study group operating within the Pentagon's Research & Development Board (RDB) and headed by Dr. Vannevar Bush. Although the name of the group is not given, proponents argue that these documents remain the most compelling evidence that such a group did exist. There is also some testimony from a few government scientists involved with this project confirming its existence.

## 21 NASA

The **National Aeronautics and Space Administration** is an agency of the United States government, responsible for the nation's public space program. NASA was established on July 29, 1958, by the National Aeronautics and Space Act.

In addition to the space program, it is also responsible for long-term civilian and military aerospace research. Since February 2006 NASA's self-described mission statement is to "pioneer the future in space exploration, scientific discovery, and aeronautics research."

## 22 The U.N.

The **United Nations UN** is an international organisation whose stated aims are to facilitate co-operation in international law, international security, economic development, social progress and human rights issues. The UN was founded in 1945 to replace the League of Nations, to stop wars between nations and to provide a platform for dialogue.

There are now 192 member states, including almost every recognised independent state. From its headquarters on international territory within New York City, the UN, and its specialised agencies decide on substantive and administrative issues in regular meetings held throughout the year. The organisation is divided into administrative bodies, primarily:

The General Assembly (the main deliberative assembly);

The Security Council (decides certain resolutions for peace and security);

The Economic and Social Council (assists in promoting international economic and social cooperation and development);

The Secretariat (provides studies, information, and facilities needed by the UN);

The International Court of Justice (the primary judicial organisation).

## 23 Edwards Air Force Base

**Edwards Air Force Base** is a United States Air Force base located on the border of Kern County and Los Angeles County, California in the Antelope Valley. It is 6 nautical miles (11 km) southwest of the central business district of Edwards, California and 7 miles (11 km) due east of Rosamond.

The base is strategically situated next to Rogers Lake, an endorheic desert salt pan; its hard playa surface provides a natural extension to Edwards' runways. This large landing area, combined with excellent year-round weather, makes the base a perfect site for flight testing.

Designated as the Air Force Flight Test Center (AFFTC), Edwards is home to the United States Air Force Test Pilot School and NASA's Dryden Flight Research Center. Almost every United States military aircraft since the 1950s has been at least partially tested at Edwards, and it has been the site of many aviation breakthroughs as a result.

## 24 The Disclosure Project

The Disclosure Project is a nonprofit research project working to fully disclose the facts about UFOs, extraterrestrial intelligence, and classified advanced energy and propulsion systems. The project has over 400 government, military, and intelligence community witnesses who have testified to their direct, personal, first hand experience with UFOs, ETs, ET technology, and the cover-up that keeps this information secret.

On Wednesday, May 9th, 2001, over 20 military, intelligence, government, corporate and scientific witnesses met at the National Press Club in Washington, DC to establish the reality of UFOs or extraterrestrial vehicles, extraterrestrial life forms, and resulting advanced energy and propulsion technologies. The weight of this first-hand testimony, along with supporting government documentation and other evidence, will establish without any doubt the reality of these phenomena. The 2001 event was filmed and reported to the media, but was not reported on the News extensively. This event will become one of the most important events in history. It was the first time that comprehensive testimony from very credible witnesses had been given about aliens and UFOs. The world's media brushed over it and should be deeply ashamed of themselves for this. One day we will look back on this event and ask, how could our media organisations have let us down by not making this conference headline news all over the world?

## People

### 40 Bob Lazar

Bob Lazar is an American scientist who currently runs a scientific supplies business in New Mexico. He came to fame in 1989 when his story hit the news. He claimed to have worked for the U.S. Navy at a secret facility known as S4 in the Nevada desert. His claims were so sensational that there was much media attention (and much scepticism). He claimed that he was recruited to work on alien vehicles which the government had (or have) in their possession. There were 9 vehicles in total, and Lazar worked on one of them. He describes the alien craft thus,

"It's very plain, it's all one solid colour, a greyish pewter colour, the same colour as the outside of the craft. There are no sharp corners anywhere. Every device in the craft, the seat, the amplifier housings, everything has a rounded corner on it almost as if it was all fashioned out of wax and then slightly melted so everything is curved. Even where the ceiling meets the floor everything has a curve to it. Very plain, very wide open, very practical use of space. There are 3 levels. The lower level houses the amplifiers themselves that swing, the 3 of them. The centre level is where you enter the craft where the seats are, and the top level is a small area and I did not have access to that so I don't know what's up there."

"Absolutely alien craft, there's no question about it. Well first of all the scope of the project was to back engineer it. If they were United States craft we wouldn't be going backward trying to find out how they were built if we had built them. Second of all, the size of the equipment inside, the size of the seats, the materials that were in use were completely alien to us (pardon the pun), and the fuel, element 115 essentially non-existent. All these factors together and of course the briefing information stating that they were alien craft."

Bob was put through a lie detector test to determine if he was telling the truth and passed. The police officer who conducted the test is quoted as saying "If he's lying, he ought to be in Hollywood".

Many people tried to discredit Lazars story, saying that there was no record of him attending the educational establishments he claims to have attended. Bob claims that when he left his employment, the government erased records in order to discredit him.

Lazar made many other claims, some of which are discussed throughout this book. One key thing to note, is that his story has never changed in 20 years and he still holds true to it today.

## 41 Phil Schneider

Phil Schneider was a geologist and structural engineer who worked on U.S. government projects building large underground military bases all over the U.S. and throughout the world. He was extremely well paid and high ranking with a top level security clearance.

Schneider ceased his employment with the government in 1979 after an incident where he nearly lost his life in a confrontation with aliens. In late August of 1979, Schneider was assigned to build an underground base in New Mexico underneath the Archuleta Mesa (a baron, desert-like area). The first task in building this type of base is to dig 4 very deep bore holes, in this case two and a half miles deep! Once the holes had been drilled, Phil would be lowered down the hole in a basket to examine the rock formation. He would then determine from his knowledge of Geology whether the rock was suitable for blasting and what type of explosives could be used on the rock. In this particular instance, the equipment being used to dig one of the holes kept coming up broken, and there was also strange soot and odours coming out of the hole. Schneider was lowered down the hole in a basket as a human observer to find out what was going on. He stumbled across an alien civilization and was met by 7 foot tall alien Grays who unleashed a blue beam which blasted his fingers off, opened his chest cavity and damaged his foot. He was saved by a soldier who was accompanying him. The soldier dragged him back into the basket and pushed the button to send Schneider back up to the surface. What followed was a fire fight between the Large Gray aliens and American troops. Schneider claims that 66 troops died in this incident.

Thomas Castello also describes a confrontation which occurred in 1979 at the same location. His account is slightly different in that he claims that there was a confrontation deep in the underground base for the control of certain areas in which aliens and American forces were involved. One possibility to explain the slight differences in their stories is that the Government knew about the conflict going on beneath the Earth in the base and as part of their strategy to gain control decided to access the lower levels by digging a hole on top of it. So Schneider was not fully aware of the reasons why the hole was being dug. He was told he was building another underground base, but all along the Government were using him to gain access to the deepest levels of the base where a conflict had been happening. It stands to reason why they didn't tell him there was a conflict otherwise he may well not have agreed to dig the holes and risk his life in the process.

After the incident Schneider contracted cancer due to the radiation that accompanied the aliens blue beam. He left his employment and did not mention his story publicly until 1995. A colleague who he had worked with was murdered for going public about this story. This is what spurred Schneider to go public with his story in 1995. He started travelling around the U.S. organising lectures, many of which were videoed and are available to watch on the internet telling his story about the confrontation with aliens. In these lectures he would give details about the Black Budget and how much money was being spent on building underground bases.

Schneider was murdered in early 1996, strangled with a piece of rubber pipe. There were many suspicious circumstances surrounding his death. Many believe that the shadow government murdered him to prevent him spreading information about the alien agenda.

## 42 Robert Collins

Robert Collins served in the U.S. Air Force in the fields of Avionics, Ground Communications, Engineering Physics and Intelligence, gaining an in-depth understanding of many career fields. After 22 years he left public service to pursue the subject of UFOs full time living on Air Force retirement supplemented by odd jobs. In his many adventures within the Air Force he was turned onto the world of UFOs by Ernie Kellerstrass in 1985. Ernie was a retired Air Force Lieutenant Colonel who worked at the FTD (Foreign Technology Division) until retiring. After performing some research he concluded that the government UFO cover-up was real and went to great lengths to uncover the cover-up which he claims spans over 60 years.

Collins claims that after the Roswell crash in 1947, one alien from the craft survived, and was "housed" by the U.S. government. He also claims that 3 different ETs lived in secret facilities in the United States at various times.

The "E.B.E." is what the U.S. military refer to extra terrestrials and stands for "Extraterrestrial Biological Entity".

Quotes from Robert Collins,

> "'EBE 1' was recovered in 1947 and taken to a containment area in Los Alamos. A voice box was put in its throat so it could communicate."

128

"'EBE 2' (1964-1984) came as part of an exchange program from the third planet of Zeta 1, and resided in a Los Alamos safe house."

"'EBE 3' was a female that arrived in 1978 and left in either '89 or '93. Reagan supposedly had meetings with two of the EBEs."

Collins has also talked about an incident known as "Gate 3" in which a "cloned biological entity" escaped a containment area in Area 51 and was subsequently shot, after the entity "pulverized" a guard.

## 43 Thomas Valone

Thomas Valone is the founding member of New Energy Congress and is an engineering physicist with 25 years of experience in emerging energy sciences. He is a Consulting Fellow of the World Innovation Foundation and has several books and 100 articles in print. He received a PhD in General Engineering from Kennedy-Western University and a Masters in Physics from the State University of NY at Buffalo.

Los Alamos national laboratory physicist Peter Milonni wrote a book entitled, *The Quantum Vacuum*, and Academic Press published it in 1994. Having read this book Thomas Valone decided it was time to do his own Ph.D. thesis on the topic Milonni's book dealt with - zero point energy. Dr. Valone did write his Ph.D. thesis on the feasibility of using zero point energy to do useful work. He more recently decided to write a separate book to make the information accessible to the layperson. Valone's new book, *Zero Point Energy: The Fuel of the Future* has as its premise that soon we'll be able to use ZPE (his shorthand for zero-point energy) to power cars and houses.

## 44 Clifford Stone

Clifford stone was a sergeant in the U.S. Army and claimed that he was a direct participant in situations involving the recovery of downed extraterrestrial crafts, some of which housed extraterrestrial beings. According to Sergeant Stone, the U.S. Government actively worked to suppress the crashed saucer recovery effort by issuing threats and orders regarding the penalties for discussing these events which Sergeant Stone witnessed on that fateful day in Pennsylvania, 1969.

Stone claims to have seen living and dead extraterrestrials while working for an Army team that retrieved crashed ET crafts.

"You have individuals that look very much like you and myself, that could walk among us and you wouldn't even notice the difference"

He then went on to add that 57 species of extraterrestrial origin have thus far been catalogued.

## 45 Thomas Castello

Thomas Castello was the senior security technician at the Dulce Alien Base. His job involved communicating with aliens on a daily basis. If there were any problems that involved security or video camera's, he was the one they called.

Castello fled his job and then released "The Dulce Papers" which include details of the 7 level, two and a half mile deep alien base where he worked. He fled the U.S. fearing his life and is believed to have been murdered.

Castello gave much information about the types of alien residing at Dulce, their interests, their characteristics, and the hierarchical structure they have there.

# 46 Stanton Friedman

Friedman graduated from the University of Chicago, earning a Bachelor of Science (1955) and Master of Science (1956) degree in nuclear physics. Friedman used to bill himself as "The Flying Saucer Physicist" due to his nuclear physics degrees. He currently refers to himself as a "scientific ufologist".  He was employed for 14 years as a nuclear physicist for such companies as General Electric, General Motors, Westinghouse, TRW Systems, Aerojet General Nucleonics, and McDonnell Douglas where he worked on highly advanced, classified programs on nuclear aircraft, fission and fusion rockets, and various compact nuclear power plants for space applications. Since the 1980s, he has done related consultant work in the Radon-detection industry. Friedman is a member of the American Nuclear Society, the American Physical Society, the American Institute of Aeronautics and Astronautics and AFTRA.

In 1970 Friedman departed full-time employment as a physicist to pursue the scientific investigation of UFOs. Since then, he has lectured at more than 600 colleges and 100 professional groups in 50 states, 9 provinces, and 16 foreign countries. Additionally, he has worked as a consultant on the topic. He has published more than 80 UFO related papers and has appeared on hundreds of radio and television programs. He has also provided written testimony to Congressional hearings and appeared twice at the United Nations.

He is the original civilian investigator of the Roswell UFO incident and supports the hypothesis that it was a genuine crash of an extraterrestrial spacecraft.  His publications regarding Roswell have been critiscised by skeptics, but his meticulous investigation has produced convincing evidence, including sworn statements by eye-witnesses and government documents to support his conclusions. Friedman has also been critiscised by skeptics for refusing to accept that all of the Majestic 12 papers are fakes, although he has found evidence that some are hoaxes.

Friedman has critiscised the scientific SETI program to search for extraterrestrial life, and has successfully debated against its director on the extraterrestrial hypothesis. He has also threatened those who have slandered him with legal action.

In 1968 Friedman argued to a Committee of The House Of Representatives that the evidence suggests that earth is being visited by intelligently controlled extraterrestrial vehicles. Friedman also stated he believed that UFO's sightings were consistent with magnetohydrodynamic propulsion - a technology that may be feasible in the near future, consistent with his (possibly since abandoned) theory that UFO's were visitors from relatively nearby in space, requiring much less advanced technology than starfaring UFOs would need.

## 47 Bob Dean

**Robert O. Dean** is a retired command Sergeant Major in the US Army who became notable in Ufology circles after he claimed to have viewed top secret documents detailing alien activity on Earth. He now lectures in Ufology around the world and has been described as an "elder statesman of the UFO community".

Dean is also notable for having successfully sued his employer under anti-discrimination laws on the ground that they were treating him unfairly because of his belief in UFOs.

In 1964, Dean claims that a U.S. Air Force Colonel, Frank Collins, gave Dean, a Command Master Sergeant, a copy of a document called "An Assessment". There were only 15 copies; one was kept in the safe. Dean said he read it every chance he had. He claims he was able to access the document because he had "Cosmic Top Secret Clearance". Dean has been unable to provide a copy of this document.

The document "An Assessment: An Evaluation of a Possible Threat to Allied Forces in Europe", stated by Dean to have been published in 1964, was one and a half inches thick, and is alleged by Dean to have been a secret NATO report on UFOs. The document was accompanied by 8 1/2 inches of Annexes and Appendices.

The report, Dean says, was ordered to be compiled by British Air Marshall Sir Thomas Geoffrey Pike, Deputy SACEUR [Deputy Supreme Allied Commander Europe] from August 1963 until his retirement in 1967. The report was prompted by a Red Alert event that is claimed to have happened on 2nd February 1961 at 0200 hrs. A formation of approximately 50 flying disc-shaped objects flew at very high altitudes, at very high speeds under intelligent control. They came from the east, flew over Germany, France, England and continued north until they disappeared over the Norwegian Sea.

The titles of some of the annexes of the report, Dean states, were as follows: Radar and Electromagnetic Effects, Optical and Light Analysis, Photographic and Holographic Analysis, Historical Research and Historical Evidence, Metallurgical and Technical Analysis, Atmospheric Physics and Meteorology, Biological Analysis and Autopsies, Sociological Problems, Psychological Problems, Theological Implications, and Worldwide Effect.

"The Assessment", Dean states, concluded in 1964 that there were 4 different extraterrestial civilisations visiting Earth but by the time of Dean's retirement from the military in 1976, he claims, there were 12 different extraterrestrial civilizations visiting Earth.

## 48 Philip J. Corso

After joining the Army in 1942, Corso served in Army Intelligence in Europe.  In 1945, Corso arranged for the safe passage of 10,000 Jewish World War II refugees from Rome to Palestine.  During the Korean War (1950-1953), Corso performed intelligence duties under General Douglas MacArthur as Chief of the Special Projects Branch of the Intelligence Division, Far East Command. One of his primary duties was to keep track of enemy prisoner of war camps in North Korea. Corso was in charge of investigating the estimated number of U.S. and other United Nations Prisoners of War held at each camp and their treatment. At later hearings of the Senate Select Committee on POW/MIA Affairs, Corso provided testimony that many hundreds of American POW's were abandoned at these camps. Corso was on the staff of President Eisenhower's National Security Council for 4 years (1953-1957).

In 1961, he became Chief of the Pentagon's Foreign Technology desk in Army Research and Development, working under Lt. Gen. Arthur Trudeau. When he left Military Intelligence in 1963, Corso became a key aide to Senator Strom Thurmond. In 1964, Corso was assigned to Warren Commission member Senator Richard Russell Jr. as an investigator into the assassination of John F. Kennedy.

Corso relates in his book "The Day After Roswell" (co-author William J. Birnes) how he stewarded extraterrestrial artifacts recovered from a crash at Roswell, New Mexico in 1947. According to Corso, the reverse engineering of these artifacts indirectly led to the development of accelerated particle beam devices, fibre optics, lasers, integrated circuit chips and Kevlar material.

In 1947, according to Corso, a covert government group, MJ12 was assembled under the leadership of the first Director of Central Intelligence, Adm. Roscoe H. Hillenkoetter. Among its tasks was to collect all information on extraterrestrial spacecraft. The US administration simultaneously, publicly discounted the existence of flying saucers, Corso says.

Corso further relates that the Strategic Defense Initiative (SDI), or "Star Wars", was meant to achieve the capability of killing the electronic guidance systems of incoming enemy warheads and disabling enemy spacecraft, including those of extraterrestrial origin.

## 49 Wernher von Braun

**Wernher von Braun** was a German rocket physicist and astronautics engineer, who became one of the leading figures in the development of rocket technology in Germany and the United States. Wernher von Braun is sometimes said to be the preeminent rocket scientist of the 20th century.

In his 20s and early 30s, von Braun was the central figure in Germany's pre-war rocket development program, responsible for the design and realisation of the deadly V-2 combat rocket during World War II. After the war, he and some of his rocket team were brought to the United States as part of the then secret Operation Overcast. In 1955, 10 years after entering the country, von Braun became a naturalised U.S. citizen.

Von Braun worked on the American intercontinental ballistic missile (ICBM) program before joining NASA, where he served as director of NASA's Marshall Space Flight Center and the chief architect of the Saturn V launch vehicle, the superbooster that propelled the Apollo spacecraft to the Moon. He is generally regarded by his supporters as the father of the United States space program, both for his technical and organisational skills, and for his public relations efforts on behalf of space flight. He received the 1975 National Medal of Science.

## 50 Zecharia Sitchin

Zecharia Sitchin is an author of books promoting the ancient astronaut theory for human origins. He attributes the creation of the ancient Sumerian culture to the Annunaki (or Nephilim) from a planet named Nibiru in the solar system. He asserts that Sumerian mythology reflects this view.

Sitchin was born in Baku, Azerbaijan, and was raised in Palestine. He acquired a knowledge of modern and ancient Hebrew, other Semitic and European languages, the Old Testament, and the history and archeology of the Near East. Sitchin graduated from the LSE, University of London, majoring in economic history. A journalist and editor in Israel for many years, he now lives and writes in New York. His books have been widely translated, converted to braille for the blind, and featured on radio and television.

According to Sitchin's interpretation of Sumerian cosmology, there is a hypothetical planet which follows a long, elliptical orbit, reaching the inner solar system roughly every 3,600 years. This planet called Nibiru  It is a planet associated with Marduk in Babylonian cosmology. Nibiru collided catastrophically with Tiamat, another hypothetical planet that was between Mars and Jupiter. The collision formed the planet Earth, the asteroid belt, and the comets. Tiamat, as outlined in the Enûma Elish, is a goddess. According to Sitchin, however, Tiamat may have been what we now know as Earth. When struck by one of planet Nibiru's moons, Tiamat split in two. On a second pass Nibiru itself struck the broken fragments and one half of Tiamat became the asteroid belt. The second half, struck again by one of Nibiru's moons, was pushed into a new orbit and became today's planet Earth.

Sitchin's supporters maintain that it would explain Earth's peculiar early geography due to cleaving from the celestial collision, that is, solid continents on one side and a giant ocean on the other. While this is consistent with the giant impact hypothesis for the origin of the Moon, that event is estimated to have occurred 4.5 billion years ago.

According to Sitchin, Nibiru was the home of a technologically advanced human-like extraterrestrial race (called the Anunnaki in Sumerian myth) who were called the Nephilim in the Bible. He claims they first arrived on Earth probably 450,000 years ago, looking for minerals, especially gold, which they found and mined in Africa. These "gods" of the Anunnaki were the rank and file workers of the colonial expedition to earth from planet Nibiru. Sitchin believes the Anunnaki genetically engineered Homo Sapiens as slave creatures to work their gold mines by crossing extraterrestrial genes with those of the Homo Erectus. Sitchin claims ancient inscriptions report that human civilization in Sumer of Mesopotamia was set up under the guidance of these "gods", and human kingship was inaugurated to serve as an intermediary between the Anunnaki and mankind. Sitchin believes that fallout from nuclear weapons used during a war between factions of the extraterrestrials is the "evil wind" that destroyed Ur around 2000 BC (Sitchin himself claims the exact year is 2024 BC), as recorded in the Lament for Ur. Sitchin claims that his research coincides with many biblical texts, and that the biblical texts come originally from the Sumerian writings of their history.

When Sitchin researched his books, only specialists could read the Sumerian language, but now anyone can check his translations in the 2006 book Sumerian Lexicon. Sitchin's translations of both individual words and of larger portions of ancient texts are considered by his critics to be frequently incorrect.

Sitchin has also claimed that certain unusual human genes discovered in 2001 were not the result of horizontal gene transfer from bacteria as concluded by geneticists (these genes could have been transferred to bacteria from humans as well), but were instead inserted into the human genome by aliens. The research itself was challenged shortly after it was published.

## 51 Nikola Tesla

Nikola Tesla was an inventor, physicist, mechanical and electrical engineer. Born in Smiljan, Croatian Krajina, Austrian Empire, he was an ethnic Serb subject of the Austrian Empire and later became an American citizen. An example of Tesla's views regarding his ethnic origin is the quote "I'm equally proud of my Serbian origin and my Croatian homeland." Tesla is best known for his many revolutionary contributions in the field of electricity and magnetism in the late 19th and early 20th century. Tesla's patents and theoretical work formed the basis of modern alternating current electric power (AC) systems, including the polyphase power distribution systems and the AC motor, with which he helped usher in the Second Industrial Revolution. Contemporary biographers of Tesla have deemed him The Father of Physics and the man who invented the twentieth century and "the patron saint of modern electricity".

After his demonstration of wireless communication (radio) in 1894 and after being the victor in the "War of Currents", he was widely respected as America's greatest electrical engineer. Much of his early work pioneered modern electrical engineering and many of his discoveries were of groundbreaking importance. During this period, in the United States, Tesla's fame rivaled that of any other inventor or scientist in history or popular culture, but due to his eccentric personality and unbelievable and sometimes bizarre claims about possible scientific and technological developments, Tesla was ultimately ostracized and regarded as a "mad scientist". Never having put much focus on his finances, Tesla died impoverished at the age of 86.

## 52 Billy Meier

Billy Meier is a citizen of Switzerland and self-claimed alien contactee. He is also the source of many controversial photographs of objects claimed to be UFOs. Meier claims regular contact with extraterrestrials, and presents much spiritual and philosophical information from these meetings. He describes the Plejaren as humanoid much like the humans of Earth.

A farmer born in the town of Bulach in the Swiss Lowlands, Eduard "Billy" Meier claims that his first alleged extraterrestrial contacts occurred in 1942 at the age of five with an elderly extraterrestrial human man named Sfath. Contacts with Sfath allegedly lasted until 1953. From 1953 to 1964 Meier's alleged contacts continued with an extraterrestrial human woman named Asket. Meier claims that after an 11 year break, contacts resumed again (beginning on January 28, 1975) with an extraterrestrial human woman named Semjase the granddaughter of Sfath.

In his teens, Meier joined the French Foreign Legion but says he soon left and returned home. He traveled extensively around the world pursuing spiritual exploration, covering some 42 countries over 12 years. In 1965 he lost his left arm in a bus accident in Turkey. In 1966 he met and married a Greek woman, Kalliope, with whom he has 3 children. The nickname "Billy" came by way of an American friend who thought Meier's cowboy style of dress reminded her of "Billy The Kid". This anecdote was told by Meier, himself, in an interview with Bob Zanotti of Swiss Radio International in June, 1982.

Meier has created a large collection of controversial photographs. He claims these photos show spaceships (called beamships) as well as extraterrestrials (humans called the Plejaren). Meier says that the Plejaren gave him permission to photograph and film their beamships in order to produce some of the evidence for extraterrestrial visitation.

## 53 Al Bielek

Al Bielek claims to have met with aliens, and worked on secret projects and ventures. He worked for various military contractors, and in the process they began to reveal secrets about extraterrestrials and psychological operations.

He was recruited into a secret project named "Montauk" and claims that he traveled on a secret underground magnetic levitation train from Los Angeles to Montauk in New York.

In January 1988, his memories of his participation in the Philadelphia Experiment started to return. Bielek made the decision to go public with the information about his involvement at Montauk and the Philadelphia Experiment in 1989. Since then he has been a frequent speaker on radio programs and conferences.

## Incidents

### 60 Cattle Mutilations

Reports of mutilated cattle first surfaced in the United States in the early 1960s when it was allegedly largely confined to the states of Pennsylvania and Kansas. The mutilations remained largely unknown outside cattle raising communities until 1967, when the Pueblo Chieftain Newspaper in Pueblo, Colorado published a story about a horse named Lady who was mutilated in mysterious circumstances. This story was then picked up by the wider press and distributed nationwide; this case was also the first to feature speculation that extraterrestrial beings and unidentified flying objects were somehow associated with mutilation.

By the mid 1970s, mutilated cattle were reported in 15 states, from Montana and South Dakota in the north, to New Mexico and Texas in the south.

Democratic senator Floyd K. Haskell contacted the FBI asking for help in 1975 due to public concern regarding the issue. He claimed there had been 130 mutilations in Colorado alone.

You might think that these mutilations are made by wild animals, or even humans having a prank. Think again. The following are some of the characteristics of tens of thousands of cases:

Presence of incisions and cuts across the body that appear to have been made by a surgical instrument, the removal of eyes, udders and sexual organs, the removal of the anus to a depth of around 12 inches, the removal of the tongue and/or lips and the removal of one ear. The stripping of hide and flesh from the jaw and the area directly beneath the ear and the removal of soft organs from the lower body. Unexplained damage to remaining organs, but no sign of damage to the surrounding area. A lack of predation signs (including teeth marks, tearing of the skin or flesh, or animal footprints) on or around the carcass. In most cases mutilation wounds appear to be clean, and carried out surgically. Mutilated animals are usually, though not always reported to have been drained of blood, and have no sign of blood in the immediate area or around their wounds.

Mutilations which have been analysed under microscope reveal incisions so precise that no technique developed by man could match the accuracy of the cut.

There are often sightings of black vehicles hovering in the vicinity of cattle mutilations.

## 61 Hudson Valley Sightings in 1982

A series of UFO sightings that took place during the eighties and early nineties. They resulted in thousands of reports of similarly-shaped UFO's. They were first observed by a retired policeman in Kent, New York, late on New Year's Eve in 1981. The "Incident at Indian Point" (a nuclear power plant) in 1984 was also one of the Hudson Valley Sightings. The sightings were all very similar. A V-shaped row of lights connected by a solid object of some type. Literally hundreds of witnesses would see the craft. There was definitely something unusual going on in the skies over the Hudson Valley. Something that moved ever so slowly and silently.

## 62 Stephenville Sightings in 2008

On January 8, 2008, Stephenville gained national media attention when dozens and later hundreds of residents reported observations of unidentified flying objects. According to reports, residents observed several types of UFOs, the descriptions ranging from triangular looking craft to discs. Several residents described the crafts as the size of a football field, while others said they were nearly a mile long. Some observers reported military aircraft pursuing the objects.

CNN's Larry King covered the story in the days following the incident, and according to Steve Allen, a private pilot who witnessed the UFO, the object was travelling at high rate of speed at 3,000 feet in the air. Allen said it was "about a half a mile wide and about a mile long. It was humongous, whatever it was."

On January 23, after initially denying that aircraft were operating in the area, the US Air Force said they were conducting training flights in the Stephenville area that involved 10 fighter jets. The Air Force said they were F-16 Fighting Falcon jets. Angelia Joiner, who during this period was the Stephenville Empire-Tribune reporter covering the story, left the paper because they ceased covering the topic. Washington Post blogger Emil Steiner reported that her termination may have been related to pressure from the Stephenville town fathers.

## 63 Illinois Sightings 2000

Here is a report from police officer Craig Stevens on this sighting,

"On January 5, 2000 at approximately 4:28am 1, Officer Craig A. Stevens was on Patrol in the Village of Millstadt. I was monitoring radio traffic when I heard a report via CENCOM, that the Highland Police Department had a report of a large object flying in the air. CENCOM dispatched Lebanon P.D. to respond. I heard Lebanon state, is the guy 10-55. Later I heard Lebanon state that he observed the object, and that it headed in the direction of Shiloh, and to have Shiloh P.D. be on the look out for it. I then heard that Shiloh had spotted the object."

"I drove to the east end of town to see if I could observe the object. Then I drove to the north end of town, in the Liederkranz Park parking lot. While I was sitting there I observed a very large flying object coming from a southward direction. The object was flying very low from 500 to 1000 ft., and was flying very slowly. The object was making no noise. I could only hear a very low decibel buzzing sound. Then the object began banking to the north east direction, and continued to cruise away from me toward the area of Dupo."

"I contacted dispatch, and advised them that I had spotted the object. I exited the patrol car, and took the Polaroid camera from the trunk, and attempted to take a picture. The camera was very cold. The temp was only approximately 18 to 20 degrees outside, and the picture did not seem to exit the camera properly."

"I heard Dupo P.D. advise CENCOM that they quite possibly observed the object, but it was at a very high altitude. I returned to the station, and drew a rough sketch of the object, and typed a report of my observations."

## 64 Phoenix Sightings 1997

The Phoenix sightings or Phoenix Lights, sometimes referred to as "the Lights over Phoenix", is the popular name given to a series of optical phenomena and sightings that took place in the sky over the U.S. states of Arizona and Nevada, and the Mexican state of Sonora on March 13, 1997. Lights of varying descriptions were seen by thousands of people between 19:30 and 22:30 MST, in a space of about 300 miles, from the Nevada line, through Phoenix, to the edge of Tucson. There were 2 distinct events involved in the incident: a triangular formation of lights seen to pass over the state, and a series of stationary lights seen in the Phoenix area. Although the United States Air Force (USAF) identified the second group of lights as flares dropped by A-10 Warthog aircraft which were on training exercises at the Barry Goldwater Range in southwest Arizona, some who observed the events believe differently. Notable among those who reported they had observed a huge carpenter's square-shaped UFO, having lights or light emitting engines, is

Arizona Republican Governor at the time of the incident, Fife Symington.

## 65 O'Hare International Airport Sighting 2006

The **Chicago O'Hare UFO sighting** concerns a multi-witness sighting of a saucer or disc-shaped UFO over Chicago O'Hare International Airport on November 7, 2006, that eventually garnered national media attention.

At approximately 4:30 p.m. on Tuesday November 7, 2006, federal authorities at Chicago O'Hare International Airport received a report that a group of 12 airport employees were witnessing a metallic, saucer-shaped craft hovering over gate C-17.

According to eyewitness reports, the strange object was first spotted by a ramp employee who was "pushing back" United Airlines flight 446 which was departing Chicago for Charlotte, North Carolina. The ramp worker then apprised the flight crew of UA446 of the existence of the spinning, metallic object above their aircraft, and it is believed that both the pilot and co-pilot of this aircraft also witnessed the object at that time.

According to Jon Hilkevitch of the Chicago Tribune in an interview on CNN's Glenn Beck program: "The disk was visible for approximately 2 minutes and was seen by close to a dozen United Airlines employees, ranging from pilots to supervisors, who heard chatter on the radio and raced out to view it." The UFO was then seen to suddenly accelerate straight up through the overcast skies. Witnesses reported that the object left behind an open hole of clear air in the cloud layer and that the mysterious hole disappeared or "closed" within a few minutes. So far, no conclusive photographic evidence of the UFO has surfaced although it was reported to Hilkevitch that one of the United Airlines pilots was in possession of a digital camera at the time of the sighting and may have photographed the event.

## 66 Roswell UFO Crash 1947

The **Roswell Incident** involved the recovery of materials near Roswell, New Mexico, USA, on July 7, 1947. The United States military maintains that what was recovered was a top-secret research balloon that had crashed. Many believe the wreckage was of a crashed alien craft and that the military covered up the craft's recovery. It likely ranks as the most famous UFO incident.

On July 8, 1947, the Roswell Army Air Field (RAAF) issued a press release stating that personnel from the field's 509th Bomb Group had recovered a crashed "flying disc" from a ranch near Roswell, sparking intense media interest. Later the same day, the Commanding General of the Eighth Air Force stated that, in fact, a weather balloon had been recovered by RAAF personnel, rather than a "flying saucer." A subsequent press conference was called, featuring debris said to be from the crashed object that seemed to confirm the weather balloon description. The case was quickly forgotten and almost completely ignored, even by UFO researchers, for more than 30 years. Then, in 1978, Ufologist Stanton T. Friedman interviewed Major Jesse Marcel, who was involved with the original recovery of the debris in 1947. Marcel expressed his belief that the military had covered up the recovery of an alien spacecraft. His story circulated through UFO circles, being featured in some UFO documentaries at the time. In February 1980, The National Enquirer ran its own interview with Marcel, garnering national and worldwide attention for the Roswell incident.

Additional witnesses and reports emerged over the following years. They added significant new details, including claims of a large military operation dedicated to recovering alien craft and aliens themselves, at as many as 11 crash sites, and alleged witness intimidation. In 1989, former mortician Glenn Dennis put forth a detailed personal account, wherein he claimed that alien autopsies were carried out at the Roswell Base.

# 12. References

Tom Valone, Review by journalist Jeane Manning from Atlantis Rising, June, 2007

Wikipedia, various pages

The Day After Roswell (Philip Corso, co-author William J. Birnes)

Disclosure Project Website

Bob Lazar Website

Protect and Survive Government Manual

Michael E. Salla Website, Exopolotics.org

Interview with Thomas Castello published on websites

Interviews with Clifford Stone published on websites

The Phil Schneider lectures

Coast to Coast AM Radio Programme and website

Quotes from President Eisenhower and Ronald Reagan speeches

UFO Evidence website

Thomas Valone lectures

Lloyd Pye television interview

Gordon Brown
The Prime Minister
10 Downing Street
London
SW1A 2AA                                                    11th August 2008

Dear Gordon Brown,

On 23rd July 2008, Dr. Edgar Mitchell who was the 6th man to walk on the moon spoke
on a British radio station. He is a highly respected scientist and astronaut.

Here are some exerts of what he said.

> "I happen to be privileged to be in on the fact that we have been visited on
> this planet. The UFO phenomenon is real although it's been covered up by
> governments for quite a long time."

> "The Roswell crash was real and a number of other contacts have been real
> and on going."

> "It's been well covered up by all of our governments for the last sixty years
> or so."

> "They are little people that look strange to us."

I would be very grateful if you could answer some very real concerns I have,

> **Do you believe that the British people have the right to know if our world
> has been contact by alien civilisations?**

> **Do you or any member of the British Government have any knowledge
> or information about what Dr. Edgar Mitchell was talking about?**

> **Do Dr. Mitchell's comments concern you and have you taken any steps to
> find out about what he was saying?**

I look forward to your response,

Yours sincerely,

*Richard D. Hall*

Richard D. Hall

To date I have not received a reply to this letter. Any reply
will be posted on the Richplanet website www.richplanet.net.

George W. Bush
The President
The White House
1600 Pennsylvania Avenue NW
Washington, DC 20500                             11th August 2008

Dear George Bush,

On 23rd July 2008, Dr. Edgar Mitchell who was the 6th man to walk on the moon spoke
on a British radio station. He is a highly respected scientist and astronaut.

Here are some exerts of what he said.

> "I happen to be privileged to be in on the fact that we have been visited on
> this planet. The UFO phenomenon is real although it's been covered up by
> governments for quite a long time."

> "The Roswell crash was real and a number of other contacts have been real
> and on going."

> "It's been well covered up by all of our governments for the last sixty years
> or so."

> "They are little people that look strange to us."

I would be very grateful if you could answer some very real concerns I have,

> **Do you believe that the public have a right to know if our world has been
> contacted by alien civilizations?**

> **Do you or any member of the American Government have any
> knowledge or information about what Dr. Edgar Mitchell was talking
> about?**

> **Do Dr. Mitchell's comments concern you and have you taken any steps to
> find out about what he was saying?**

I look forward to your response,

Yours sincerely,

Richard D. Hall

To date I have not received a reply to this letter. Any reply
will be posted on the Richplanet website www.richplanet.net.